Southern
Illinois
University
Press

James Joyce's Pauline Vision:

Southern Illinois University Press: Carbondale and Edwardsville

A Catholic Exposition

Robert Boyle, S.J.

FEFFER & SIMONS, INC.: LONDON AND AMSTERDAM

Dedicated with love to the memory of
William T. Noon, S.J., and Mabel Worthington

Library of Congress Cataloging in Publication Data

Boyle, Robert, 1915–
   James Joyce's Pauline vision.

   Includes bibliographical references and index.
   1. Joyce, James, 1882–1941—Religion and ethics.
2. Christianity in literature.   I. Title.
PR6019.09Z52618   823'.9'12   78–18901
ISBN 0–8093–0861–4

Copyright © 1978 by Southern Illinois University Press
Printed in the United States of America
Designed by David Ford

Contents

Foreword

"Man is but an Asse"

When my cue comes, call me, and I will answer. My next is, most faire *Piramus*. Hey ho. *Peter Quince*? *Flute* the bellowes-mender? *Snout* the tinker? *Starveling*? Gods my life! Stolen hence, and left me asleepe: I have had a most rare vision. I had a dreame, past the wit of man, to say what dreame it was. Man is but an Asse, if he goe about to expound this dreame. Me-thought I was, there is no man can tell what. Me-thought I was, and me-thought I had. But man is but a patch'd foole, if he will offer to say, what me-thought I had. The eye of man hath not heard, the eare of man hath not seen, mans hand is not able to taste, his tongue to conceive, nor his heart to report, what my dreame was. I will get *Peter Quince* to write a ballet of this dreame, it shall be called *Bottomes Dreame,* because it hath no bottome; and I will sing it at the latter end of a play, before the Duke. Peradventure, to make it the more gracious, I shall sing it at her death.—*Midsummer Night's Dream* (act 4, first folio)

Stephen, discussing "Hamlet, I am thy father's spirit" (*U* 188), hears two personalities in that "I": the voice of buried Denmark and the voice of unburied Stratford—not John Shakespeare but William, the creator of Hamlet Senior. Similarly, I hear two voices in the passage above: that of the incomparable Bottom, brooding over the mysterious "dream" of being embraced by a fairy queen; and that of the author of *MND* itself. This second voice expresses the purpose of Shakespeare, much larger than Bottom's. Bottom is using the Pauline text to find some expression of the experience he foggily recalls; Shakespeare further uses it to express the wonder of the "strange and admirable" in human love and folly. For him too St. Paul's wonder at the embrace of God for asinine humans makes a useful comparison.

Maybe, the text seems to hint, human love, as it does in Sonnet 116, can overcome time and even death, at least in a dream.

The Pauline stress on God as master of death itself (central in Hopkins's *The Wreck of the Deutschland*) may be felt in Bottom's intention of deriving grace for his song from Thisbe's death. Or perhaps he means that the singing of his ballad, like Falstaff's babbling of green fields, will add grace to her death.

Having wakened, Bottom first busily frets over his operation as principal actor (like "Burbage, the young player" [*U* 188]), and, finding himself deserted, contemplates and then tries to express the ineffable experience he dimly recalls. He moves into relatively solemn diction ("most rare vision") and philosophical insight ("past the wit of man") as he recalls the strange and admirable scene on "a bank where the wild thyme blows." He is probably thinking of himself when he says "Man is but an Asse," realizing, in his present struggle to conceptualize so mysterious, "strange," and practically incredible an event, how impossible exposition of a human experience (at least so rare a vision) clearly is! Still, he tries, with his repeated "me-thoughts," and decides that only a patch'd fool (like Jaques' "motley fool," or like Buck Mulligan, "blithe in motley" [*U* 197]) would attempt to reach into those strange areas of the brain, or of the heart.

Now Bottom vents in mangled form the sublime passage in which Paul attempts to express the Christian dream. Paul wants to expound for the Corinthians, faced with a "wisdom of this age" not unlike that which the complacent and rationalistic Theseus will propound in act 5 of *MND,* the "secret and hidden wisdom" of God's infinite love. As Bottom will turn to Peter Quince for expression, Paul turns to Isaiah, who long before had implied the yearning of ear and eye straining to hear and see the hidden, loving God. "From of old no one has heard or perceived by the ear, no eye has seen a God besides Thee, who works for those who wait for him" (Isa. 64:4). Paul, anxious to stress the incomprehensible and rationally incredible belief that the Infinite Being wished to embrace so crass an animal as man, paraphrased the great Prophet's words: "But, as it is written, 'What no eye has seen, nor ear heard, nor the heart of man conceived, what God has prepared for those who love him' " (I Cor. 2:9). This, he goes on to say, we know through the Spirit of God, who alone comprehends the thoughts of God. Man must be content, as Paul and theologians following him well knew, with apprehension. These words, in theological context, indicate the difference between the grasp of ultimate mysteries proper to the mind of God, and the lack of grasp which the limited mind of man can reach.[1]

Bottom, in his frustrated effort to express the beauty and inexplicable ecstasy of having his own ass ears stroked by "divine" fingers, turns to the passage he had heard in church as a classic expression of the strict mystery of God's love for man. He confuses eye and ear because words are difficult for him, more skilled at weaving cloth, and perhaps because the changes he has felt in his own head and tongue and honest heart have confused him more than ordinarily. Further, in Sonnet 23, in the context of "an unperfect actor on the stage," Shakespeare had urged that his books (perhaps his own Quincian ballads) should do what, overcharged with love, his heart and tongue could not do. He urges the synaesthesia which Bottom demonstrates, the mixing of functions of eye and ear: "O, learn to read what silent love has writ. To hear with eyes belongs to love's fine wit."

Having turned to Paul for some kind of expression, Bottom thinks of turning to Peter Quince, a poet and playwright, who will perhaps, by some miracle "in black ink" (Sonnet 65), be able to express some apprehension of the dream. He has already observed that it is past man's wit, so that he can find now a special metaphysical reason for calling that poem *Bottomes Dream* (as his creator calls his own poem *A Midsummer Night's Dream*). And, continuing in the Pauline atmosphere so neatly set up in his own comparisons of the dreamer with the theologian with the prophet with the poet, all dealers in ineffable mystery, focusing on the "strange" rather than on the factual and familiar "true," he sees, as Paul did, the fullness of grace as the beautifier and loving conqueror even of death.

Behind or above that projected voice of Bottom I hear the true voice of Shakespeare the great ventriloquist, the dramatist hidden like the god of creation, expressing some of his own insights and attitudes. He is in Bottom, "all in all" (*U* 212), and can respond to a cue. He knows, as well as James Joyce does, how to turn religion, and all other human things, to his literary ends. His own most rare vision of foolish mortals, in apprehension like gods yet gross as weeds, "such stuff as dreams are made on," goes past his own wit to expound, though not, by incomprehensible miracle, to express. I suspect that he addresses literary critics, college men perhaps, or at least learned and dogmatic judges like his friend Ben, when, tongue in cheek, he forms the words "man is but an Asse." The expounders of dreams attempt to comprehend and dissect those visions which the poet, like the lunatic and the madman and the prophet, can experience and which the poet can at least in some measure express.

When Shakespeare turns to Paul, he has in mind an analogy between the religious mystery which is Paul's concern and the literary mystery which is his own concern. Bottom himself is involved in a play dealing with Greek myth which parodies the play in which it appears, and that play is written by Quince, an anachronistic Christian carpenter, himself a parody of the humorous builder of the play expressive of a summer's dream, the vision of a man not yet shaken badly by the cold winds of winter. Shakespeare too will sing his dream before a queen, and he knows, as he reveals in Sonnet 65, that after that queen's death and his own, his vision will by a human miracle shine bright and gracious in a naughty world.

I find no difficulty in perceiving Shakespeare to be thus responsive to Paul's effort to express the inexpressible. Shakespeare's use of the Bible has received ample study (though, as I will hint later, maybe not enough), and his supposed religious attitudes have been wrested in all conceivable directions, among others by Stephen's (and Joyce's) dean of studies, Father Darlington. All I see here is that Shakespeare is, like Joyce, using Paul's text to make a literary point of his own—namely, that literature like Scripture deals with visions (which may be had by asses as well as Magi), and that the miraculous and inspired expression of them may not be totally subject to the rational dissection of nonpoets.

The Pauline passage in question has received attention from practically every writer on Scripture, and draws literary artists with magnetic force. Two of those I am concerned with in this book, the true Jesuit, Gerard Hopkins, and the self-styled Jesuit, James Joyce. Hopkins uses the passage as directly as Shakespeare does, paraphrasing it in stanza 26 of the *Deutschland*. In his search for the reasons behind the nun's cry of "Christ, Christ, come quickly," Hopkins is wondering in this stanza whether it might not have come from a desire for relief from suffering, as the heart is cheered by spring after a long winter of "moo-cow" low-uddered clouds. Or, thinking of that glorious spring sky first in the daytime, then at night, with the humid night fruit of the stars (like those that glow over the back-garden of 7 Eccles Street), he recalls Paul's text—

> Blue-beating and hoary-glow height; or night, still higher,
> With belled fire and the moth-soft Milky Way,
> What by your measure is the heaven of desire,
> The treasure never eyesight got, nor was ever guessed what for the hearing?

This denotes merely that this controlled Heraclitean fire (like a belled cat, I take it, the image involving both the warning bell for the ear and the mystic patterning of the celestial fires for the eye) makes a good analog for the beauty of heaven; but it connotes, in its larger context, that the very mystery which Paul celebrates, the mystic embrace of God, is the real answer to Hopkins's question, "The majesty! what did she mean?"

Joyce uses the text less explicitly than does Hopkins, so that it is, I suppose, possible to wonder whether he uses it at all. My own conviction—that the Pauline text shines out from *FW* 482: "What can't be coded can be decorded if an ear aye sieze what no eye ere grieved for"—may seem at first glance to require some relatively esoteric circumstances: a mind conditioned by the numerous elements of *Midsummer Night's Dream* in *FW*; a Catholic alertness to the religious profundities of the text; a philosopher's sensitivity to its metaphysical implications; a consideration of Joyce's constantly deeper use, and his decreasingly acrimonious toleration, of religious and specifically Catholic doctrines and attitudes to express his own literary theory and practice; and other elements. Maybe so. My own judgment is that what I see is actually present in Joyce's text, and not merely in my own reading of it. But even if it is not, if the text was not even subnesciously[2] in Joyce's mind when he wrote those words, I consider that the evidence I intend to bring to bear upon my perception of the text will, in illuminating Joyce's total product, justify my procedure. Such illumination, at any rate, is my aim. Even if I do exaggerate (or altogether project) Joyce's use of the Pauline text that Shakespeare and Hopkins and I (with some millions of others) have found so significant, the faint path which leads to that nondefinitive conclusion will, I trust, display enough oases of literary beauty to make the long desert journey, even without a satisfactory epiphany at the end, of interest and value.

I figure that I have seen in Joyce's work a most rare epiphanic vision, and that, like Bottom, I consequently have difficulty in expressing what I have seen. Still, I intend to try, since I have a strong hope that some others do or can see it too. This is a human hope, I am aware, founded on a human faith, not on rational certitude. But I am all the more satisfied with it, myself, because the older I get the more flimsy I discover rational certitude to be. And I do have enough experiential certitude to balance my hope upon, enough for this book, anyway. I aim at those who, like Bottom, can accept apprehension with all its puzzles and incertitudes and ultimate questioning. Those who, like Theseus, look for comprehension, with questions chosen to fit rational answers, with no risky toe-dippings into the void, are advised to look elsewhere. But then, I tend to feel, as I see it from my own angle, they would do better to avoid Joyce, Hopkins, and Shakespeare too.

Joyce, at any rate, has no hesitation in becoming a Shakespearean ass. In chapter 13 of *FW,* one outstanding voice is that of the ass, sounding out from Anastashie's bower. That bower is either identified with or compared to Titania's canopied bank, protected by the fairies' warning, "Come not near." The man under that arch, with the strange wrinkling nose, breaks into speech with "methoughts" like Bottom's, and describes the most rare vision, also in biblical tone ("And lo"), of Shaun, vested from top to toe, like the ghost in *Hamlet,* in correct wear. This ass does better than Bottom in expressing and even in expounding his vision, though he prefaces his exposition, on *FW* 405, with what I take to be a reference to Bottom's "Man is but an Asse." Having adverted to his lack of the wisdom of the Evangelists, he offers, in his tinker's way, the literary tinkle (with overtones of both bells and urine) of his low-keyed braying: "Had I the concordant wiseheads of Messrs Gregory and Lyons alongside of Dr Tarpey's and I dorsay the reverend Mr MacDougall's, but I, poor ass, am but as their fourpart tinckler's dunkey."

With full asinity he sets out to expound the dream, in Palestrinian four-part counterpointing ("no purer puer palestrine e'er chanted panangelical" [*FW* 407]). Principally he proceeds by drawing forth from the lips of the Vision (i.e., Shaun) the exposition of Shaun's intention to write the Gospel that,

Shaun claims, Shem could not write. Mr. Atherton's problem with "ambly andy" seems to me solved by considering that Shem (as the voice of the Ass) is acknowledging Shaun's intention of being both Saviour (thus a *successful* Hamlet) and the true asinine Dreamer (thus a triumphantly expository Bottom).[3] Whatever Shem aims to be, Shaun claims to be that and better (as Buck did with Stephen). But I see no sign that Shaun as epiphanic vision in his "spacest sublime" ever actually succeeds in changing roles with Shem, who alone can "beat time."

In the Vision's opening revelation, which begins on *FW* 407, he expresses his excessive concern for his twin, which develops at the top of page 409 into what seems to be an assertion, once again, of his own superiority, as Eye, over his brother, as Ear (as the spacious Ondt will pontifically put down the time-eating Gracehoper). The Vision's Catholicism has striking similarities to that of Mrs. Kernan in "Grace": "Her beliefs were not extravagant. She believed steadily in the Sacred Heart as the most generally useful of all Catholic devotions and approved of the sacraments. Her faith was bounded by her kitchen but, if she was put to it, she could believe also in the banshee and in the Holy Ghost" (*D* 171–72). Shaun links the Banshee with Shem, I believe, and the Sacred Heart with himself, as, unlike Bottom who confused ear and eye, he asserts their separation—helpful to a hypocritical rationalist: "But, Gemini, he's looking frightfully thin! I heard the man Shee shinging in the pantry bay. Down among the dustbins let him lie! Ear! Ear! Not ay! Eye! Eye! For I'm at the heart of it" (*FW* 409).

Shem is, as he pointed out on *FW* 194, down among the dustbins in a coalhole, "to me unseen blusher in an obscene coalhole," where in his ear he can pick up the low things as he listens to the heartbeat of humanity. Shaun poises ready for an eyeful as he ascends into heaven. Shakespeare, in his own manipulation of Bottom's paraphrasing of St. Paul's "eye" and "ear," had added (most significantly, I think) the report that the tongue gave to the deeply knowledgeable imaginative heart's commonsense interpretation of what the five senses reported—perhaps as the five clowns (who themselves are named with some relation to the senses) are to be lifted to the level of tragedy by Peter Quince, whose designation "carpenter" is so closely associated in Latin with Joyce's favored "artificer." Joyce like Bottom's creator well knows the value of shifting eye to ear when it can be done, as Tom and Huck found it convenient to shift identities.[4]

This epiphanic vision comes at midnight, the zero hour, and the bells of the old church mingle with the heartbeats of sleep to form this counterpointed music. Tied up with Scripture, as in the *Book of Kells* (*kil* is *church* in Gaelic), the "book of kills," counterpointing as on the "*Tunc* page" Greek and Roman crosses, fire-breathing monsters with the loving Christ, the *Dio Boia*, perhaps, of the Romans (with Father Dolan and the Grand Inquisitor hovering near) and maybe burned Bruno (like Greek Stephen Dedalus and the crucified

Christ)—some of such similarities and contraries float through Joyce's most rare vision: "He is cured by faith who is sick of fate. The prouts who will invent a writing there ultimately is the poeta, still more learned, who discovered the raiding there originally. That's the point of eschatology our book of kills reaches for now in soandso many counterpoint words. What can't be coded can be decorded if an ear aye sieze what no eye ere grieved for" (*FW* 482). These climactic bells chiming from the old church carried my mind back to the bells which united Stephen and Bloom at their climactic parting and brought them different but deeply linked and counterpointing messages. In this context, Bloom's "Heighho" identified itself in my imagination with Bottom's "Hey ho," and Stephen's liturgical chant allied itself in ghostly union to Hamlet's "Angels and ministers of grace." I have tried, in this book, to reconstruct some of the experiences of many years past which have brought me to my present view (an unstable one) of *Finnegans Wake* and of Joyce's catholic vision. My attempt to express my view in terms of Joyce's use of Catholic doctrines, practices, and attitudes does not quite hit the target, but since the target itself, like everything else involved, keeps dissolving and shifting—"every person, place and thing in the chaosmos of Alle anyway connected with the gobblydumped turkery was moving and changing every part of the time" (*FW* 118)—I decided just to take what aim I could and let fly. Something may land, and, if not, my own feeble shakes of the "collideorscape" may make an attractive pattern here and there.

Milwaukee, Wisconsin   Robert Boyle, S.J.
October 1977

List of Texts Used and Abbreviations

Chamber Music, CM

James Joyce. *Chamber Music.* Edited by William York Tindall. New York: Columbia University Press, 1954

Stephen Hero, SH

Theodore Spencer, ed. New York: A New Directions Book, 1963

A Portrait of the Artist as a Young Man, P; *Dubliners, D;* *Exiles, E*

The Portable James Joyce. With an Introduction and Notes by Harry Levin. New York: Penguin Books, 1976

Ulysses, U

New York: Vintage Books, Random House, 1961

Finnegans Wake, FW

New York: The Viking Press, 1963

Letters, 1, 2, 3

Letters of James Joyce. Vol. 1 edited by Stuart Gilbert, vols. 2 and 3 edited by Richard Ellmann. New York: The Viking Press, 1966

Ellmann

Richard Ellmann. *James Joyce.* New York: Oxford University Press, 1969

James Joyce's Pauline Vision

1 Mad Winthrop's Delugium Stramens

In the First Watch of Shaun, chapter 13 of *Finnegans Wake,* a most rare vision appears. Two obscure figures, one a man with an apparently nonhuman nose, the other the world's most beautiful woman, observe the apparition from a bower protected, like Titania's, by the fey admonition "Come not nere!" Bottom's "like any suckling dove" has apparently here been applied to the sexual advances of the lovely woman, whose black lips (a reflection, no doubt, of the Queen of Sheba, allied to the "dove" of Solomon's Song of Songs) seem to have served Titubante with the reverential adoration Bloom brought to Molly at the end of "Ithaca."

The voices that emerge, in this text, from the many levels of the Dreamer, circulate about "like them nameless souls" (*FW* 410), the "multiple Mes" of the Speaker, or of one of the speakers. Joyce's text differs from Shakespeare's, where two voices are readily distinguishable, and from Hopkins's, where only one voice clearly appears, because Joyce's method allows the free emergence of all voices that haunt the dreamer's conscious, subconscious, and subnescious levels. Thus we must, as in dreams, sort out what we can of the many shifting ghosts who, as if on the dark embattled arches of Elsinore, troop to the call of the Artist, the Stephen-Hamlet, the "Bous Stephanoumenos" (*U* 415).

In this chapter, the place (or one of the places) is near "the belfry of the cute old speckled church," near the Liffey and the washerwomen's laundry (*FW* 403–4). The bell tolls the zero hour, and it is on the stroke of twelve, not yet struck, since the first listener (the "Hark!" probably emerges from the woman) hears six sounds, numbers in varied languages, and the second listener ("Hork!" comes from under that gorsecone cap) hears five. Perhaps the varied languages indicate that we all ("it was when you and they were we" [*FW* 403]) are identified with this primal pair, whatever our actual place or language. We are, after all, as in Shakespeare's dream play, "in nonland of where's please" (*FW* 403).

This "kirkeyaard" in which the odd pair lies seems to me identical with that on *FW* 201-2, where "Heighho" (the message Bloom received from St. George's bells) and "Heehaw" (the ass's cry, like that Bloom heard in Glasnevin churchyard, and thought of his own lonely father) enclose a description of four persons, "Grandfarthring nap and Messamisery and the knave of all knaves and the joker" (*FW* 202). Those four, HCE and ALP, and Shem ("her knave arrant" [*FW* 229]) and Shaun ("Jem is joky for Jacob" [*FW* 169]) are present in the bedroom, the father and mother actually (if one may use such an adverb of a dream), and the sons (emerging or emerged from the parents) as present in the picture over the mantel. As the four watches of Shaun develop into the last one, we see more clearly the setting which is so obscure on page 403. The man and woman are in bed, and "Over mantelpiece picture of Michael, lance, slaying Satan, dragon with smoke" (*FW* 559). The "Mark as capsules" (*FW* 403) may be a stage direction allied to "Chamber scene. Boxed" (*FW* 559). "Capsule" is from the Latin word for "box," and thus the phrase may mean, "Set off in boxlike fashion."

As the nymph from over Bloom's bed descends in incense in the hallucinating "Circe" scene in *Ulysses,* so in chapter 13, Mick and Nick descend from the picture, Nick (or Shem) to identify for once with the creative father (and with Nick Bottom), and Mick (or Shaun) to emerge, like Christ from Mary, as an epiphanic vision. The whole chapter, a rehearsal ("as his general address rehearsal" [*FW* 407]) for what will be repeated in the later watches, seems to be reversals of expected roles, shiftings and deceptions somewhat along the line of those in the "Eumaeus" of *Ulysses.* The father and mother do not operate (except perhaps in their own dreaming), and the sons carry the action, Shem as the ass speaking for the four old men and as Bottom speaking for Shakespeare, Shaun as the phony ideal artist, allied to Christ, to Hamlet, to Puck (who deceived through the eyes), to Buck Mulligan (who is also Puck, *U* 215).

With some hesitation and humility, Shem attempts to set forth the most rare vision of "Shaun in proper person" (*FW* 405). He presents a parody of the Perfect Hero involved in the four Gospels (especially as they come to us in the *Book of Kells*), in Shakespeare's art, in Hopkins's art, and especially in *Finnegans Wake* itself. "Whom we dreamt was a shaddo, sure, he's lightseyes, the laddo!" (*FW* 404). The "shadow" for Shakespeare is an actor, "a walking shadow," and, as Stephen's treatment of Hamlet and the ghost suggests, more substantial than a "real" person. "The light of the eyes" seems to be a paraphrase of "the light of the world," a most special "laddo," and the passage here recalls to me another context loved by the young Joyce. In Yeats's "Rosa Alchemica," Michael Robartes speaks of the gods who "are always making and unmaking humanity, which is indeed but the trembling of their lips." And he speaks of visions of those gods: "There is Lear, his head still wet with the thunderstorm, and he laughs because you thought yourself an existence who are but a shadow, and him a shadow who is an eternal god."[1] Puck, in the epilogue of *MND,* in similar Yeatsian mood, voices Shakespearean irony in contrasting "we shadows" and "visions" with the solid "reality" in the burgher streets outside the Globe Theatre. Yeats in Wildean vein urges the doctrine, opposite to that of Theseus, that the higher life is in the imagination. From the tone of Shem's description of the "shaddo," the Yeats meaning operates along with that Shakespearean one of which Robartes too is conscious. Robartes probably voices the view of his creator in his implied ridicule of those who think themselves, as real flesh and blood, superior to Lear the "shadow," who is the true reality, the formless spiritual essence (as AE puts it, *U* 185). That it is here spelt "shaddo" reveals the presence of Joyce the grinning mature Dreamer who would find the whole Blavatsky crowd more than a bit fishy.

In Shem's dream vision "methought broadtone was heard" (*FW* 404), as in the opening etherial chords of Mendelssohn's overture ("There's Mumblesome Wadding Murch cranking up to the hornemoonium" [*FW* 377]), and then come to his large ears in Mendelssohnian fairy rhythms "the creepers and the gliders and flivvers of the earth breath and the dancetongues of the woodfires and the hummers in their ground all vociferated echoating: Shaun! Shaun! Post the post!" (*FW* 404).

The vision clears gradually, and as Shem waits for the voice of the visitant, the overture sounds again: "Overture and beginners! When lo (whish, O whish!) mesaw mestreamed, as the green to the gred was flew, was flown, through deafths of durkness greengrown deeper I heard a voice, the voce of Shaun, vote of the Irish, voise from afar" (*FW* 407). And that voice sighted "open tireless secrets," having first signed the holy secrets with seven hand signals (like Buck's "talking hands" [*U* 17]), symbols of the sacraments:

1) "His handpalm lifted": The mass and Eucharist, as in Stephen's musings in *P* 420: "No touch of sin would linger upon the hands with which he would elevate and break the host."

2) "his handshell cupped": Baptism

3) "his handsign pointed": Confirmation

4) "his handheart mated": Matrimony

5) "his handaxe risen": Penance, with a faint echo of King Hamlet, and somewhat allied to Bloom's musings: "Confession. Everyone wants to. Then I will tell you all. Penance. Punish me, please. Great weapon in their hands" (*U* 83).

6) "his handleaf fallen": Extreme Unction, with some echo of Macbeth's "the sere, the yellow leaf."

7) "Helpsome hand that holemost heals! What is het holy!": Holy Orders, allied also to Bloom's "More than doctor or solicitor" (*U* 83).

"It gested": refers to the matter of the sacrament, the ritual symbolic action, as the pouring of water. "And it said": refers to the form of the sacrament, found in the words spoken by the minister of the sacrament. Cf. Stephen, *P* 358: "If a layman in giving baptism pour the water before saying the words is the child baptised?"

In my own context, which may not be Joyce's, I cannot help but observe that the two elements which the artist Shakespeare added to St. Paul's passage as paraphrased by Bottom, "Mans hand is not able to taste" and the "report" of the heart, are stressed in these artistic hand signs of Shaun, especially in "handheart matched."

Shaun goes on to claim that his revelation comes from St. Columcille, "Hagios Colleenkiller's prophecies" (*FW* 409). The *Book of Kells* has already been well established by Shaun, in the voice of Professor Jones (*FW* 122), as a source of revelation and of literature—and a cryptic prophecy follows: "After suns and moons, dews and wettings, thunders and fires, come sabotag. *Solvitur palumballando!*" (*FW* 409).

Every day of the week leads up to this "sabotag" or "shoe-day," appropriate to the postman, and a day ambivalently a holy sabbath and a sabotaging witches' sabbath. This last leads into the Latin pun, which, building upon the familiar response to Zeno's problem with space, "Solvitur ambulando," introduces a number of old and new themes with "palumballando," which literally means "by stakedancing." A *palum* was a post or stake around which soldiers trained, and it had a phallic significance in classic writing. Thus the maypole dancing of the rainbow girls comes in, with echoes of chapter 9 and some preparation for the girls of chapter 14. Also, the "leaping nimbly" (*U* 19) of Buck Mulligan, as he capered to his own phony ascension, fits into the numerous echoes of "The Ballad of Joking Jesus" which surround the Shaun of this chapter.[2]

"Ambly andy" in the line following "palumballando" is formed out of the expected "ambulando," and may be Shem's hint to Shaun to cease the dancing, especially around a pole, if he expects to complete the Way of the Cross and arrive at his rehearsal for his ascension. "Salve a tour" could also, besides suggesting "salvator" and foot-salve, suggest in Latin and French (i.e., "goodbye in turn") "Goodby, now, goodbye" from "The Ballad of Joking Jesus." The phrase "Top, Sid, and Hucky," besides the interesting exchanging of personalities among Mark Twain's characters suggested by Atherton, echoes, in what Shaun is telling them ("for my vacation in life") the Ballad's "tell Tom, Dick, and Harry I rose from the dead."

Shaun also compares himself, like Stephen waking to produce his villanelle, to the Blessed Virgin, recalling the angel's words to Mary at the Annunciation, "The Holy Spirit will come upon you, and the power of the Most High will overshadow you" (Luke 1:35). Shaun says "and there does be a power coming over me that is put upon me from on high out of the book of breedings" (*FW* 409–10). Shaun thus draws the Blessed Virgin into his visionary appearance, suggesting that his shining forth is allied to the scene of Bethlehem and his own role, displacing Shem, as "some god in the manger" (*FW* 188).

The feminine and Marian aspect of this bower and vision scene which opens chapter 13 is stressed more in one of its later reappearances, beginning on page 501. The scene is somewhat clearer, in this later stage of the dream—the levels in the dreamer have shifted somewhat, the orbits have revolved a bit, there's been a shake to the "collideorscape" (*FW* 143), the inkhorn has traveled (*FW* 118), or however one wishes to imagine it. But here we are again, with a silence instead of the bells, maybe that same silence before the stroke of twelve, or maybe some later point in time. We are reenacting "a particular lukesummer night" (Luke alone has the Nativity scene), where "the isles is Thymes," where glimmering bonfires now stream to the heavens, where our lord is ghosting himself and our lady of the valley is still murmuring, no doubt still in lowdelph. There is rain and dew, and in this context the advent hymns' celebrating Christ as dew join the Liebestod suggestions. The whole of page 502 is sprinkled with Christmas hymns, familiar especially in the milieu Joyce knew, as in the "Lo, how a rose ere blooming, A tender branch has sprung! A rose from root of Jesse, as prophets long had sung. It bore a flower bright, that blossomed in the winter, when half-spent was the night." The suggestions of Mary in "holy-as-ivory" and in "jesse" prepare us for "jusse as they rose and sprungen," hinting that very young Joyce in his school choir at Christmas had sung the hymn, as we did in my choir, also in the lovely German.

> Es ist ein Ros entsprungen
> aus einer Wurzel zart,
> wie uns die Alten sungen:
> von Jesse kam die Art
> und hat ein Blümlein bracht
> mitten im kalten Winter
> wohl zu der halben Nacht.

And two lines later, the most famous of all Catholic Christmas hymns, the original "Come-all-ye," the "Adeste Fideles, laete triumphantes," appears somewhat modified perhaps by camel rhythms, with a touch of Jabberwock motion, into "Lieto galumphantes." Four lines above, there is indication that in East and West, in the whole Catholic church, this "naissance" is celebrated—"westnass or ostscent." "Gales, westnass or ostscent" may bring to a willing mind the gifts of gold, incense, and myrrh which the Magi brought West from the East; and the Pentecostal gusting of gales, blowing where they will ("allin humours out of turn"), will alert Catholics to that Power which came upon Mary in the Annunciation, celebrated thrice daily in the Angelus, and which came upon her also (in Catholic tradition) as upon the Apostles at Pentecost—and which is even now coming upon Shaun.

As with the clowns in *Midsummer Night's Dream,* there is much concern about whether the moon shone "that highlucky nackt" (as there was concern in Bethlehem about a star). And Mary is stressed, in relation to the Annunciation, "Hail Mary, full of grace," and to Christmas itself, "Holy Mary, Mother of God"—which, perhaps owing to the "white fogbow" (*FW* 403), shifts a trifle into "smother of fog," and all of which faintly echoes Bloom's "Pray at an altar. Hail Mary and Holy Mary. Flowers, incense, candles melting" (*U* 83).

Midsummer Night's Dream appears here by name, first adapted to ALP (or Anastashie, or Mary, or Eve, however the shake of the kaleidoscope comes out), "Miss Somer's nice dream." And then adapted to HCE (as Bottom, or Shem, or the Ass), "Mad Winthrop's delugium stramens." For midsummer to change to midwinter is fitting on several grounds, principally I suppose because the Shaun-Christ vision emerges from the manger scene in this Christmassy "fall of littlewinter snow." We heard on *FW* 405 Bottom's description of the spatial "holy messonger angels" nudging holy Shaun on toward his winding way of the cross, and the Epiphanic "blueblacksliding constellations," guides to the Wise, shaping the temporal windings of Shaun's watches. Now in terms of the wilder aspects of Shem-Bottom's own vision, on *FW* 502, we find the dream turned into a nightmare of delirium tremens. But not that either, since it really is "delugium stramens," a deluge of straw, a most happy situation for an ass! This neatly echoes Bloom's practical dream, an agricultural one, containing cows and "1 pike of upland hay" (*U* 715), after "sowing hayseed, trundling . . . newmown hay" (*U* 714-15). He could speak about a straw for hours, according to the narrator of "Cyclops" (*U* 316), not only as a Jew whose forebears lacked straw for bricks[3] but, it may well be, as an ass who yearned for straw rather than for the new nuts which Titania offered to Bottom.

The play in *FW* now takes on a development allied to but quite different from that of chapter 13, but before it goes far, the spot itself on which the pair lies gets a significant name: "This stow on the wolds, is it Woful Dane Bottom?" On *FW* 430 the schoolgirls were attracted "to the rarerust sight of the first human yellowstone landmark," the most rare vision, the perfumes that emerged "of wild thyme and parsley." This "stow on the wolds" of *FW* 503, one with the bower of *FW* 403, is also the source for those wild thyme odors, since it coalesces with the bank where Puck found the lovely Titania and where she embraced the translated Bottom. But why "Woful Dane"? Hamlet as the supreme hero and Bottom as the supreme clown are both, as Stephen sees the matter, Shakespeare. And Bloom too, in the possibilities which life held for him (as I shall touch on later), could have followed the example of the actor most famous as a Hamlet or the actor famous as a Shakespearean clown. This spot of vision, the stage for Shem's (and HCE's) rare vision, involves the limits of human grief and of human laughter, the profoundest soundings of human experience, Christmas and the Way to Calvary, and is thus well called "Woful Dane Bottom." At least so I speculate.

When we run into the name in the last chapter, "warful dune's battam" [*FW* 594], the fog is nearly gone. We're nearly ready for towel and warm water, and the sun will soon break through, it seems. And since a resurrection seems to be getting closer, it is no great surprise to find here, not far from the bed which has served as the Dublin equivalent of the bank where Bottom and Titania acted out a Pauline dream, a quotation from a resurrection poem written in Dublin, when Joyce was six years old, "That Nature is a Heraclitean Fire and of the comfort of the Resurrection" by Gerard Manley Hopkins.

> Across my foundering deck shone
> A beacon, an eternal beam. Flesh fade, and mortal trash
> Fall to the residuary worm; world's wildfire, leave but ash:
> In a flash, at a trumpet crash,
> I am all at once what Christ is, since he was what I am.

That Pauline notion of the identity of Christ and Christian—"I live now, not I, but Christ lives in me" (Gal. 2:20)—is the dream to which Bottom turned for his paraphrase, and which Joyce also uses. Here Joyce paraphrases, with a hint of the Easter pasch celebrating the resurrection to which the still sleeping pair have almost come, Hopkins's dramatic rhymes, "A flasch and, rasch, it shall come to pasch" (*FW* 594). Then Joyce picks up a specifically Jesuit image from Hopkins, which, had Hopkins lived even to his mid-fifties, Joyce could have heard from Hopkins's own lips. As it is, Joyce was hearing it often enough from other Jesuit lips, in their speaking of the central devotion of the Society of Jesus, the Sacred Heart. Hopkins's treatment of the heart in his *Deutschland* and in "The Windhover: to Christ our Lord" Joyce very likely adverts to in "by hearth leaps live" (*FW* 594) and perhaps in "swigswag, systomy dystomy" (*FW* 597). But of this I intend to speak at some length in my final chapter, in dealing with what I consider to be Joyce's most penetrating use of Catholicism, allied to Hopkins's own use of it. The difference in the way Hopkins understood "I am all at once what he is," as an objective though incomprehensible becoming another and divine person without ceasing to be himself, in supernatural union in the Mystical Body (a notion also Pauline), and the way Joyce would understand it, as the subjective way in which Shakespeare was father to his characters—

> Looke how the fathers face
> Lives in his issue, even so, the race
> Of SHAKESPEARES minde, and manners brightly shines
> In his well torned, and true filed lines

or as the way in which characters in *FW* become each other and remain fully Joyce—such difference is obvious enough. But the likeness which attracted Joyce is that, in both dreams, out of mortal trash (or out of "asch") some kind of Phoenix may spring up. For Hopkins this is certain, for Joyce it is at least a human dream, and in the "only human" universe (or chaosmos) of his art it remains that. But he does not, as some of his readers do, slam a rational door on the possibility. While he is well aware of this dream's incomprehensibility, like Bottom and like Hopkins and like Paul, he recognizes and uses its apprehensibility—or perhaps it might be closer to the truth to say that among other dreams he tolerates and uses also this one. In any case, he brings Father Hopkins into his Pauline stow in the wold, and not just to make fun of him.

The obvious differences in Joyce's and Hopkins's and Shakespeare's use of religion for their literary purposes should not be allowed to obscure the important similarity: the use of religious language, dogma, attitude, and emotion to stress the point that literature, too, essentially focuses on mystery. In religion, faith takes over where reason becomes inoperative, apprehension replaces comprehension. In literature, a common "whyacinthinous" acceptance of "unfacts," similar to Bottom's honest acceptance of an experience he could not comprehend or explain (contrasted to Theseus' crisp "more strange than true"), forms an analogue to religious faith. This important principle I find expressed fully in these three powerful artists. Shakespeare may have shared Joyce's personal distaste for religion, for all I know, but he certainly shared Joyce's knowledge of religious experience, and he showed Joyce, more than Dante did, ways of turning that knowledge to literary use.

Throughout *FW* Joyce uses Mamalujo, usually with relation to their faithful ass, and with generous elements of parody and lampoon and even bitter ridicule, to deal with matters identical with or similar to religious revelation. We have seen the ass in chapter 13 appealing to the "concordant wiseheads" (*FW* 405) of the Evangelists, who express matters of faith incomprehensible to reason, and we have listened to his asinine effort to express "objects nonviewable to human watchers" (*FW* 403). The "violet" of nighthood which renders those objects nonviewable is allied in Joyce's imagination, I judge, with the "violer d'amores" of the book's first page. Joyce told Miss Weaver that "violer" was "viola in all moods and senses"

(*Letters,* 1: 247), and in his family Italian "viola" is "violet." It is the bottom of the rainbow, the dark rainbow girl most likely to have "prayings in lowdelph," and the first touch of color as light begins to emerge from the void. "The nodding violet" grows in rhyming harmony on that magic knoll where "the wild thyme blows" (*MND* 2. 1. 250), and is, in my own recreation of Joyce's midnight vision, allied also to that "little western flower," pierced by Cupid's deflected bolt, "now purple with love's wound" (*MND* 2. 1. 167). The juice of that blossom, in the eyes, transforms any live creature into an object of love, even of mad dotage. The deception of the eyes (as, for example, the deceptions of "Puck" Mulligan [*U* 215–16], who held the cracked Wildean mirror up to Stephen's peering eyes [*U* 6]) is Shaun's whole hope; he can appear as "a goodmantrue" only under some such circumstances, similar to those effected by "love-in-idleness" in *MND*.

In any case, Joyce uses the Evangelists as Shakespeare uses St. Paul, to the end that the work of literature becomes analogous to the inspired Scripture. Only the ass-headed Bottom has the experience of being embraced by a superior being, and he judges that only the artist Peter Quince will have the wise head to express something of what Bottom's heart has known.

The heart is for Joyce, as for Shakespeare and for Hopkins, the source of truth and of poetry. Hopkins expresses this in the *Deutschland* and most of all in "The Windhover: to Christ our Lord," which I intend to discuss in my final chapter, to indicate Hopkins's kinship with Joyce in at least this aspect of Jesuit attitude toward the Sacred Heart. Distasteful as that abused devotion obviously was to Joyce, he shared with Hopkins the view that the beat of the heart was the life not only of love but of living literature, and that profounder truth comes from the heart than comes from the head. Still, as Hopkins too states in the *Deutschland,* ideally the heart and brain work together, until the heart, "hard at bay," leaps beyond the limits of reason in the assent of faith. Bottom does something analogous to that in his acceptance of the vision his brain cannot comprehend or express, as Hopkins does in his own acceptance of the nun's experience, which he too finds himself unable to express, breaking off like Bottom as his usually competent Fancy breaks down under the strain of facing the ineffable—

> But how shall I . . . make me room there:
> Reach me a . . . Fancy, come faster—
>   Strike you the sight of it? look at it loom there,
> Thing that she . . . There then! the Master,
>   *Ipse* . . .   (Stanza 28)

He abandons the effort to predicate what the brain cannot comprehend, and settles for nouns (like that Latin one, thrice repeated in the Mass, here quoted directly from "Ipse autem Dominus noster Jesus Christus . . . exhortetur corda vestra" (2 Thess. 2:15), with echoes of two others operative in the devotion to the Sacred Heart and in the final image of "The Windhover: to Christ our Lord," "qui dilexit me, et tradidit semetipsum pro me" (Gal. 2:20), and "sed semetipsum exinanivit" [Phil. 2:7]). Failing in predication, the nouns simply point at the Pauline mystery, using Paul's favorite term to signify the incomprehensible Person ("Ipse"—"Himself") who comes to embrace the nun. Joyce's ass sets himself an analogous task as he attempts to encounter and to question the shining Person who has emerged from the Dublin darkness surrounding this Dublin version of Titania's bower.

Joyce's ass, like Hopkins speaking of "heart-throe, birth of a brain" (*Deutschland,* stanza 30), wants that cooperation of "cor" and "wisehead" which might find a brighter and more expressive key for the prophet's harp than this limited "dunkey" can bray forth. He seeks a solution to Theseus' dilemma, "How shall we find the concord of this discord?" (*MND* 5. 1. 60).

Perhaps a beginning might be made by mingling eye and ear, reason and faith. Faith deals, in the basic formula attributed to St. Paul, with "the evidence of things that are not seen" (Heb. 11:1), which can be apprehended only. "For we walk by faith, not by sight" (2 Cor. 5:7), one of the ways in which Shem, who depends on ear, differs from Shaun. "So faith comes from what is heard" (Rom. 10:17), which makes the ear more important than the eye, as faith, in dealing with true mystery, is immeasurably more important than reason. This I see (by reason) as a fundamental factor in Joyce's casting Shem the artist as an ear and Shaun the rationalist as an eye. And it operates in two of the reasons why the speaker on *FW* 403 can deal with "Irish objects nonviewable to human watchers." The first reason is that, as artist, he is an ear, and thus not dependent on sight. He can, therefore, like Bottom mixing sight ("seeing" mixes with "seeming," and perhaps with "scene," in "mescemed") and hearing, cry out, "And lo, mescemed somewhat came of the noise" (*FW* 404). Through hearing he moves from "shaddo" to "lightseyes." Thus overwhelming concord may emerge from the noisy discord, and what cannot be "coded" by the mind "can be decorded if an ear aye seize what no eye ere grieved for" (*FW* 482).

On that same page, *FW* 482, ears hear the golden truth borne by soft breezes, whispering the name of the ass-eared father, similar to Midas ("Me das has or oreils"). And the wild ass belonging to John, "his onagrass," gives background to the counterpointing "bells of scandal" (*FW* 483, echoes of Father Prout's "The Bells of Shandon") which rang out scandal about the bedded pair on *FW* 139. Those bells seem to me allied to the bells ("The iron tongue of midnight hath told twelve" [*MND* 5. 1. 370]) and ears and nodding ass of chapter 13.

Shakespeare's Bottom, in his role as Pyramus, continues his suggestive synaesthesia: "I see a voice. Now will I to the chink, To spy an I can hear my Thisby's face" (*MND* 5. 1. 194). To see the word and to hear the vision might overcome some of the difficulties Bottom and St. Paul both face. Space and time could be, if not transcended, at least coalesced, and some of the limitations of human deficiency in comprehension might be diminished. The approach to human mystery in human terms might benefit if the space organ could deal with the invisible broken air flowing in and the time organ could send out beams to contact the visible outer object.

But I lose myself in the mazy text once again. The point I am attempting to cling to is that Shakespeare and Joyce operate in an ancient Catholic tradition which does express itself in bells and ears and dreams and visions, and which claims to conquer time and death. It builds on mystery, on the void of the suprarational (or sub- or even ir-), and thus, as Stephen of "Scylla and Charybdis," in the course of his heroic effort to expound Shakespeare's vision, points out, it is not subject to effective attack from rationalists: "On that mystery [of the Trinity, where the Father, alone among fathers, consciously begets his truly consubstantial Son] and not on the madonna which the cunning Italian intellect flung to the mob of Europe the church is founded and founded irremovably because founded, like the world, macro- and microcosm, upon the void. Upon incertitude, upon unlikelihood" (*U* 207). The mystery of true human love can be analogously apprehended (by faith alone) in that divine relationship between Father and Son; thus Stephen, in inflated accents, echoes Catholic insight, which asserts that love is more perfect in the Trinity than in that human perception which turns to the madonna and "amor matris" as the ultimate norm. Stephen, as I can now understand him, is attempting in his argument to discredit the Church's claim to fatherhood as the supreme symbol of love, the base for "Our Father." But the operation of the book in which Stephen exists, with the whole operation of *Finnegans Wake,* where the father rises in the closing lines to enclose the babbling mother (unless, of course, it is the other way around), still struggles with this open question. Religion, Stephen seems to be saying, tries dogmatically to settle the question, but for the artist the question remains open, whether it is love of woman or love of man (objective genitive if the love is for another, as in Shakespeare's Sonnet 116 for example, or his putative love for Mr. W. H.; subjective genitive if the love is for himself, as in Buck's gross "Everyman His own Wife") where the human spirit can find rest. Stephen, I believe, leaves no room for Augustine's answer ("You have made us for yourself, O God, and our hearts are restless till they rest in you"), but Joyce and Shakespeare, whatever their personal responses may have been, leave that possibility too richly open. They do not, like the immature Stephen, close off any possibility of development in the void of mystery. Nor do they, as artists, assert any finality. Like sensible aural Bottom and unlike dogmatic visual Theseus, they accept what they experience and express that, leaving universal comprehension and finality to human asses.

Revelation uncovers divine mystery; true literature uncovers human mystery. To uncover is not to give answers, but to "swell lacertinelazily before our eyes" (*FW* 121) with the failure to reach answers, to leave us floating in the dark chaos we somehow dimly feel to be a cosmos. Like Bottom waking to "reality," Joyce's Dreamer sometimes approaches the surface of his chaosmic experience to question and to recall human efforts to dogmatize, to schematize, to catechize. But like Bottom, he hangs on to his most rare dream even endlesslesslessly—unless it suddenly ends after a definite article.

2 To Tara via Holyhead

What echoes of that sound were by both and each heard?

By Stephen:
   Liliata rutilantium. Turma circumdet.
   Iubilantium te virginum. Chorus excipiat.

By Bloom:
   Heigho, heigho,
   Heigho, heigho.

—*Ulysses* (704)

Clive Hart, in *A Wake Newslitter* for April 1974, points out that the bells Stephen and Bloom hear at the climactic moment of their parting (and Stephen's disappearance into nonbeing) had early in the book served a useful purpose of fixing the time. At least in Bloom's case the same bells did it, and in Stephen's case Hart reasonably supposes that some clock-tower in Kingston served the purpose. The three pairs of "Heighos" in "Calypso" (*U* 70), one pair for each quarter of an hour, in the rhythm of the striking bells, indicate the time relative to the approaching funeral which haunts the mind of Bloom emerging from the jakes at 8:45 A.M. At the same moment in "Telemachus" (*U* 23), Stephen's mind reviews the first three Latin phrases above, from the prayers for the dying in the *Roman Ritual,* which Stephen arranges in three-line form, quite different from his earlier fuller and more straightforward recall (*U* 10) of those words recited over his dying mother. Hart concludes that Stephen is also arranging the phrases in the rhythm of bells he hears, and that Stephen and Bloom set out on their odysseys at 8:45

A.M. Having through the day's peregrinations finally come together, they part at 1:30 A.M.

In the morning, those bells, the actual ones that Bloom hears and the unmentioned ones that Stephen may hear (their verbal immateriality is appropriate for a Satanic semi-Platonist who intends to create his own cosmos), toll for both listeners also a message of death. Stephen thinks of a priest speaking monkwords over his dying mother as he turns from the real priest emerging from the water and from the metaphorical prelate plunging in (*U* 23). Bloom, less self-centered, notes the ghostly overtone trailing through the air, and with musical skill learned from Molly fixes its interval from the tonic, and feels sympathy with dead Dignam (*U* 70).

Things have changed in the nearly seventeen hours between the responses to the bells. Stephen has again received food, this later time not the beggar's portion of rations as in the breakfast in the tower served under the mocking sign of the Trinity, but the nourishing human and bovine gifts freely given with human love in the House of Bondage. He heard those first bells while looking forward to a day of uncertainty, of disenfranchisement and eviction, of almost hopeless struggle to survive as a teacher, a scholar, a poet, like Melchisedek with no father or mother, with no responding lover and only a Butcher God ready with a cosmic pandybat. He hears these last bells looking forward to a dawn in which there may be music. It is not recorded how in the morning he moved up the hill to Dan Deasy's school, but I am certain that his footsteps did not have then the confident reverberation and vibration which sound in the ears of Bloom: "Alone, what did Bloom hear? The double reverberation of retreating feet on the heaven-born earth, the double vibration of a jew's harp in the resonant lane" (*U* 704). In a kind of mystic vision on the beach of "Proteus" (*U* 48), Stephen had drawn from beyond the veil that covered his own sacred and adored imagination the vision of himself "in violet night walking beneath a reign of uncouth stars." He strides now, in this most vital and significant moment, as he disappears from the book and from human ken, like a man on his way somewhere, with something to accomplish.

That "jew's harp" for years caused me prosaic imaginative trouble. I used to wonder whether some insomniac in No. 5 or No. 3 Eccles was leaning from an upper window, twanging a Jew's harp into the night. I could see no obvious way to fit the sound of Stephen's feet into the narrow limits of a Jew's harp's scale, so I was pretty sure that it must be a metaphorical harp based on the reverberation of Stephen's retreating feet. Plenty of metaphorical harps prepare one. In his brooding on Fergus's song, and Fergus's ruling of the kind of disheveled wandering star Stephen is about to become, Stephen sees the waves move in "twining stresses, two by two. A hand plucking the harpstrings merging their twining chords. Wavewhite wedded words shimmering on the dim tides" (*U* 9). The cloud covers the sun as he broods on the death of his mother in terms of Fergus's "love's bitter mystery." That cloud brings to Bloom's mind too desolation and grey horror (*U* 61). Now all these hours later the sounds of Stephen's twining feet may bring to both their harmonizing minds the notion of words wedded to that narrow, simple, ancient rhythm of the brazen Jew's harp, a tiny echo of Fergus's "brazen cars" and a bridge between Fergus and David the Jew, thus a link between Celtic Stephen and Jewish Bloom.

A happy note in *Herring* 455[1] gives a clue as to Joyce's intention: "(SD bootsoles on flags of hollow lane twanged a fourfold chord, scale of a jew's mouth harp)." A twanging of a fourfold chord is the basis for the harp's coming into Bloom's mind and echoing in its own vibration the sound of those revelatory bells. Further, Joyce would most likely have known Skeat's opinion that the Jew's harp was so named in derision of David's harp, and this might have gone with his note, *Herring* 453 "(LB juvenis made fun of jews)." Bloom, or perhaps more likely Joyce, may be here contrasting the great cosmic sweep of the symbolic constellations with the small range that Stephen can effect in the Jew's lane, with an overtone of the way in which the despised music of David has in the Psalms filled the human cosmos.

The "twanged" of this note carried my mind back to Bloom's elastic band in "Sirens" (*U* 274), also "fourfold": "Love's old sweet *sonnez la* gold. Bloom wound a skein round four forkfingers, stretched it, relaxed, and wound it round his troubled double, fourfold, in octave, gyved them fast." Bloom is thinking of harps, specifically Tara's harp, in relation to himself and Boylan: "Erin. The harp that once or twice. Cool hands. Ben Howth, the rhododendrons. We are their harps. I. He. Old. Young" (*U* 271). Then Bloom's elastic harp "buzzed, it twanged. . . . He stretched more, more. Are you not happy in your? Twang. It snapped" (*U* 277). Thus Bloom is prepared, when he hears the limited reverberation and feels on his eardrums the vibration of Stephen's feet in the lane, to think of a Gaelic poet of Tara, who has just sung of a Jew's daughter sacrificing him (a religious transmogrification of the Temptress of the Villanelle) and has drunk the cream of a Jewess from the Pauline hands of "*Christus* or Bloom his name is, or, after all, any other, *secundum carnem*" (*U* 643), and to think of him therefore as also singing of the experience of the Jew with whose eyes his eyes conversed. In some such fashion can be suggested something of the background, in the depths of Bloom, that enabled him to hear "A jew's harp."

The two nouns descriptive of the sounds from Stephen's feet distinguish between time and space, it seems to me. "Reverberation" describes the beating out of time, as the fourfold chord referred to in the *Herring* note comes into being, better here than on the elastic band which buzzed and snapped. "Vibration" I take as stressing the movement of the sound, and of the harp, in space. The time element is moving away from Bloom on "retreating feet," and the space element is moving back toward him. The beats of the feet touch the lane, but the vibrations touch the responding eardrum of Bloom. The double movement both away and toward reminds me of the movement of the recumbent Bloom and Molly, which I take also to be paradoxically double: "In motion being each and both carried westward, forward and rereward respectively, by the proper perpetual motion of the earth through everchanging tracks of neverchanging space" (*U* 737). William S. Doxey sees that while the "mistake" involved, since the earth in the factual and scientific atmosphere of phenomenological "Ithaca" should be turning eastward, may be comically undercutting Bloom's confidence in science, it also may have more profound implications.[2] Doxey suggests a balance with Molly's "they might as well try to stop the sun from rising tomorrow" (*U* 782), a thing that Molly will in no sense speculate about. Joyce uses the same directional imagery throughout his work, as for example, in the conclusion of "The Dead," where Gabriel, who has been constantly tending to move east, thinks that he must face tomorrow his journey westward. The west as symbolic of death occurred to many, but it was Bernard Benstock, in his deeply perceptive study of the story, who first pointed out the connection with the epiphanic journey of the Magi, who had to make their journey westward to find the Word which brought forth all flesh.[3] Gabriel must turn toward Michael, "Who is like to God," to find the Word to which all flesh must come, all that inclusive group referred to in the Apostles' Creed (recited daily by the young Joyce) and in the concluding words of the story, "the living and the dead." The implied artist's journey to find his artistic word functions particularly well, too, in this Irish Epiphany story written about the time that the eastern Dubliners were violently rejecting Synge's western words.

Often in *FW* the west lights the east, as for example when HCE (and Joyce the Dreamer speaking through him) asserts that with wax in hand, unlike Kernan in "Grace," he will "westerneyes those poor sunuppers and outbreighten their land's eng" (*FW* 537). "The west shall shake the east awake" (*FW* 473) when brave footsore Haun finishes his *Work in Progress*. Something of the brutal rationalism from Patrick's Trinitarian east confronting the Druid's mystic and colorful west is foreshadowed in HCE's zoo, with its houyhnhm music from the west and its beastly strife from the east: "tendulcis tunes like water parted fluted up from the westinders while from gorges in the east came the strife of ourangoontangues" (*FW* 541). Tea, the symbol of the Eucharist from the East moving to the West, operates in *Dubliners* and *Ulysses,* circling especially around Tom Kernan, a role taken over in *FW* by the Tunc page with its two kinds of crosses: "there are two signs to turn to, the yest and the ist, the wright side and the wronged side" (*FW* 597). Here as elsewhere in *FW,* the west and east, like the crossed bones of the death's head and like the contraries of Bruno and like Shem and Shaun, tend to flow into one another and get mixed, and in the subnescious world at the base of *FW*'s language, accomplish more profoundly the more conscious and subconscious simultaneous and contrary motions suggested in Bloom's and Molly's moving factually east to find the dawn and metaphorically west to find the artist's newborn word where alone they can exist. The Magi journeyed west to Bethlehem and found divine life; Molly and Bloom are metaphorically journeying west to Tara to seek out the language in which they can share human existence. And all of this is akin to Stephen's walking east, as I myself imagine him doing to find the boat to Holyhead, the one way in which he, like his creator, will be able to find his way west to Tara.

Joyce's first songs were written to the music of a Jewish harp, building as Joyce's music does throughout *Chamber Music* on the Song of Songs—in his own arrangement of the poems, the climax and the exactly central poem, No. 17 of the thirty-four poems, was "My dove, my beautiful one, Arise, arise!" (No. 14 in Stanislaus's arrangement). That passionate scriptural Song, so important in Catholic devotions to the Blessed Virgin, surges to the surface in Stephen's ambivalent bringing of the Courtly Love traditions to Mary's altar in *Portrait*. The implied shaming that Skeat finds in "Jew's harp" is explicit for the Irish harp in "Two Gallants," where the central element in the powerful insight into the total perversion of Irish gallantry is most profoundly expressed in the heedless and weary harp, with her coverings fallen about her knees, a symbol of the young woman used by Corley and of degraded Ireland.

After their cocoa-communion and their liturgical urination, Bloom, who had under the influence of the night sky thought of Eastern dulcimer strings (*U* 57), plucked by the diviner, Coleridge, now hears Stephen's feet, for the first time in his life sounding confidently and resoundingly on the heaven-born earth, giving out the music of another kind of harp. In No. 26 of *Chamber Music,* the woman, putting her ear to the shell of night and divining a message, perhaps of death or of ghosts or both, from her own pulsing blood, shares the mood of the creator of Kubla Khan, who had drawn his own insight from Purchas. Now Bloom, the chanter of Hebrew and echoer of the harp of David, to whom Dante had turned for his explication of his own art, hears "the double vibration of a jew's harp in the resonant lane" (*U* 704). That tinkling music might by magic power fill the earth and heavens, and summon forth shadows more lasting and more real than flesh.

David the Dancekerl (*FW* 462) seems to me closely allied to the departing Stephen, both "a squamous runaway" and a "darling proxy" for Bloom, as Dave is for Juan. Dave operates in a eucharistic context, in "chalished drink" (*FW* 461) and "eucherised," and he will show up "in the fraction of a crust," like Christ known to the disciples at Emmaus in the breaking of the bread. Juan's "But soft!" echoes Buck's "Slow music, please" on the opening page of *Ulysses*. The relationships, particularly the Jewish ones, between the dancing David and Stephen have been discussed with great insight by Edmund Epstein,[4] and I see in the "jew's harp" image further connections between their sounding feet. A few pages later, Joyce adverts to Lewis's comparison of him to Mr. Jingle—the "jubal" may refer to the kind of dance so called; to the liturgical Latin imperative, "jube," which precedes the reading of the Catholic sacred scroll; to the jujube candy Joyce habitually associates with Africans; but above all to "the father of all those who play the lyre," Jubal of Gen. 4:21: "Could you wheedle a staveling encore out of your imitationer's jubalharp, hey, Mr Jinglejoys?" (*FW* 466). The double reverberation of a Jew's harp's jingle has worked its way, as I hear it, into the condemnation of imitators of David. The harps and griefs of Psalm 137, "By the waters of Babylon, there we sat down and wept, when we remembered Zion. On the willows there we hung up our lyres," are echoed in woes of HCE at the close of chapter 4 of *FW*: "Nomad may roam with Nabuch but let naaman laugh at Jordan! For we, we have taken our sheet upon her stones where we have hanged our hearts in her trees; and we list, as she bibs us, by the waters of babalong" (*FW* 103). The Jewish woe was identified with the Irish woe in terms of this psalm by Stephen in "Proteus," as he remembered the song of Kevin Egan exiled in Paris: "They have forgotten Kevin Egan, not he them. Remembering thee, O Sion" (*U* 44). The sacred waters of the Jordan and the Liffey and the Seine, better than the pagan Tigris and Euphrates, flow together in Stephen's imagination to unite the Irish harps with the Jewish.

Those two harps had already mixed with Catholic dogmas in one of Stephen's learned verbal constructions, at least as I can read "contrans-magnificandjewbangtantiality" (*U* 38). In "Aeolus," under the headline "O, Harp Eolian" (*U* 127), MacHugh with dental floss sounds "between two and two of his unwashed teeth" (like the "double . . . double" of the unwashed feet of Stephen, *U* 704) another "resonant" sound that apparently reaches Bloom's ear like the double twang of a Jew's harp, "Bingbang, bangbang." Stephen's word, involving "jewbang," was in the context of Arius's war on the doctrine of the Trinity and the consubstantiality of Father and Son. I used to think Stephen was working with eucharistic dogma involving consubstantial and transsubstantial in relation to the "Magnificat" of Mary celebrating the Incarnation. Then the "jewbang" could refer to the destruction of Jewish doctrine of the unity of God, or to the imagined intercourse between Mary and the Power (or Stephen's seraph coming to the Virgin's chamber or Buck's and Taxil's pigeon. That seraph of Stephen's could be imagined by him to be the Word himself, the Second Person of the Trinity, instead of the scriptural Gabriel, in line with Christ as seraph giving to St. Francis of Assisi the stigmata, celebrated in Hopkins's *Deutschland* as "seal of his seraph arrival." That would make a bit more sense of Stephen's drunken supposition of something shameful as he quotes in "Oxen" (*U* 391) Dante's *vergine madre figlia di tuo figlio)*.

But now it seems to me more likely that the whole word celebrates the Trinity, with which Arius was concerned. The "con" then would refer to the Father, basis of all the relationships; the "trans" would refer to the Word, into

Whom the divine meaning "passes" and who "passes across" into the material cosmos; the "magnificans" would refer to the Holy Spirit, who as Power "magnifies" the Word in Mary and carries the divine life into the created cosmos. Then "jewbang" would be the harp music of the Spirit tangible to the ears of Stephen and all the saved, sounding from Dublin unwashed teeth and feet.

The sorrowing voice in *FW* 103 produces "hearts" instead of "harps," which may reveal some fulfillment for the prayer of Stephen's mother at the end of *Portrait*: "She prays now, she says, that I may learn in my own life and away from home and friends what the heart is and what it feels. Amen. So be it" (*P* 526). Anna Livia has a profounder view of the artist's vocation, as she writes of the necessity of his knowing all aspects of human experience, as she notes his need for dancing, for expressing himself in musical motion: "He had to see life foully the plak and the smut, (schwrites). There were three men in him (schwrites). Dancings (schwrites) was his only ttoo feebles" (*FW* 113). Bloom hears in the limited range and relatively feeble beats of Stephen's feet a double motion which suggests to him a Jew's harp. Joyce hears a more basic and cosmic double motion, the beat and motion of the human heart, expressive of life and the individual's unique response to life: "Every talk has his stay, vidnis Shavarsanjivana, and all-a-dreams perhapsing under lucksloop at last are through. Why? It is a sot of a swigswag, systomy dystomy, which everabody you ever anywhere at all doze. Why? Such me" (*FW* 597).

In the *Herring* note, the resonance rises from the "hollow lane," which enlarges in Bloom's imagination (or in that of the speaker of "Ithaca") into "the heaven-born earth." The relationship of the earth to the sun and the stars, important in the celestial symbolism of "Ithaca" and in the turning Gea-Tellus of the last chapter, receives emphasis, but principally the relationship of the poet to woman takes a central position. The harp for the artist, as Joyce's work amply demonstrates, is climactically woman. Molly, who celebrates the dawn, and ALP, who divinizes the coming of night at the end of chapter 8 and the cosmic solar theophany at the close of the book, bring his great epics to their nonconclusions; they are his *clou* to immortality. And Molly, half Irish and (probably) half Jewish, makes the perfect harp for Stephen, as ALP makes the perfect harp for Dave-Shem. Since it will soon become clear to us that Molly herself is the heaven-born earth, the music that Stephen the determined artist strikes out from the earth can be, for those with eyes to see it that way, a symbol of the chamber music in which Joyce will create Molly.

I find in this image, also, an aspect of the Trinitarian imagery Joyce employs in his triangle of characters. Heaven and earth unite in Molly, and Stephen and Bloom, as Son and Father, unite not only in their symbolic urination but in their contemplation of each other in the light of Molly's mystery. Bloom attracts Stephen's gaze to the visible luminous sign of Molly's presence (*U* 702), and elucidates "the mystery of an invisible person." As they urinate, first Bloom the father, then Stephen the son elevate their gazes to the projected shadow, recalling the shadow of Stephen, projected beyond the stars, the self of an "unbeheld" if not invisible person (*U* 48). The shadow is luminous to the good eyes of Bloom, semiluminous to the weak eyes of Stephen. And while they urinate, the harp star proper to the poet Stephen, Vega in the Lyre, shot beyond the Tress of Berenice, here proper to Molly, toward Leo. Something of the Trinity's activity seems to be symbolized here, with the son moving from above the zenith in relation to the Spirit and the Father, as Christ might be imagined as having been sent on his salvific mission into the material cosmos, driving through the power of love to the creating father. "Mystery" is a powerful word for Joyce, with special force drawn from Catholic tradition (Avery Dulles's article on "mystery" in the *New Catholic Encyclopedia* can provide background for some of the significance the term had for Joyce), and the formality of "invisible person" invites us to respond to the Pentecostal overtones of "denoted by a visible splendid sign," as the Spirit became visible to the apostles in tongues of fire. The Father generates the Son, and together they breathe forth the Spirit. The Spirit, though invisible, is the "Power" of the sacraments, the Power that overshadowed the Virgin and effected the Incarnation, the electric power that Buck on the opening page of *Ulysses* whistled for and then ordered to switch off the current. In this way Molly is the force for both the artist Stephen, though she reaches him only through Bloom, and for the creative father Bloom, though at the moment he cannot fully express his creative drives in communion with her. Molly gives the strongest drive to the poet to express her mystery and to the father to reproduce it.

The mixture of the Trinity, the Mass, and the Eucharist operates, I believe, in the Prankquean passage, *FW* 21–23. One of the answers to her riddle, "Why do I am alook alike a poss of porterpease?" is "Because I am consecrated wine." I puzzle this out from the "I am," the name of God; from the connections with Piesporter wine, to which Tindall refers, and to Joyce's favorite amber wine, Fendant, which he habitually called the archduchess's urine;[5] from the likelihood that "poss" combines pot and piss; and because the three parts of the riddle suggest the three principal parts of the mass. A possible contributing factor to the selection of Jarl van Hoother's name, or at the least a happy coincidence in the name's structure, rises from the religious suggestiveness of the initials: they fit a Hebrew word applicable to the Father, Jahveh (transliterated Jehovah); a Latin word descriptive of the Son, Verbum; the English name for the Holy Ghost; and the J (h) V H of the Tetragrammaton—thus three persons and one nature, the Trinity.[6] Jarl as "high up" points to the Offertory of the mass, with the priest holding up in his hands the materials of the sacrifice, the bread and the wine. Jarl "drowned in his cellarmalt" suggests the Consecration, where the cold wine becomes warm blood as the priest (now God the Son) makes the wine one with himself (so to speak). Jarl "in the pantry-box," where the bread comes from, "hopping out handihap" suggests Communion, a breathing forth of Love, who is most properly the Prankquean, the goddess, Imagination. She had picked a red rose in her first foray, when she took Shaun on a trip through space, "Tourlemonde." She picked a pink rose when she took Shem on a timely tour through himself, like Hamlet reading the book of himself, "Turnlemeem." And she picked a white rose, "a blank," containing all the colors which break out in HCE. The brimming chalice of Stephen's villanelle here becomes a piss-pot of Piesporter, and an answer to the riddle is, "Because I am transaccidentated, and all you can see of me is the appearance of wine, or, in the chambermade music in which I exist, of urine." The Trinity is symbolic of all generation and regeneration, of man and woman ("everybully and ribberrobber") bringing forth children, of eye and ear bringing forth cosmos, of red and pink bringing forth white and thus all colors, of the five vowels (like the Porters at peace in this consecrated ink) bringing forth all the alliterative poetry in the Heraclitean flux of this four-elemented world ("flamend floody flatuous world") of *Finnegans Wake*. As later in Shem's eucharistic image of literature proceeding from the ink made of his urine and defecation, here the thunderword and poetry proceed from his ordure and her threefold wit.

Joyce often turns to the Trinitarian mystery in *FW* as he strikingly does on page 486, where he deals with the artist's harping of human mystery, "History as her is harped," in relation to an act of Catholic devotion. Before the reading of the gospel at mass, Catholics (some at least now, all did it in Joyce's time) made the sign of a small cross with the thumb on the forehead, the lips, and the breast. On *FW* 486, Luke applies a cross, which among other things might be a suggestive Eastern "t" like that on the Tunc page, a good basis for psychosinology, first to Yawn's temple, whereupon he *sees* a cook carrying on his brainpan a cathedral. The sign on the forehead honors the Father, so one interpretation of Yawn's vision would be the creative and planning Father operating *ex cathedra*. Applied to the lips, the sign honors the Word, and here Yawn *feels* a fine lady, perhaps Christ's Church or the Virgin herself. Applied to the breast, the sign honors the Holy Spirit, symbolized in the will, which in turn is tied up with the heart, the act and the organ of Love; here Yawn *hears* the heart itself, sounding like the Gracehoper, the swigswag, systomy dystomy common to all flesh. I take it that this marvelous passage concerns itself, as the presence of Swift and his ladies might suggest, with the operation of the literary artist descending into himself, as the Trinity might be imagined doing in God's solipsistic bliss.

As I read the passage, Joyce suggests that the Father, for artistic purposes, is the least important, that seeing and the brain are the shallowest of the activities essential to the artist's vision. The Son, dealing with feeling and with lips, reaches deeper into human experience, and can speak out perhaps most effectively in musical cries, "O la la!" The Spirit is deepest and most basic, dealing with hearing and with ear. This recalls the marvelous woman of *CM*, No. 26, who hears her own heart when she puts her divining ear to the shell (as do the sirens in their chapter in *Ulysses*), and fears the ghosts conjured up best by the magicians Coleridge and Shakespeare, inspired by the more factual Purchas and Holinshed. Thus it seems to me that Molly, as the invisible and to shallow sight, it may be, seemingly the least important of the Ulyssean trinity, actually is the true power of the book, and the goal to which all its mind and lips (Leopold and Stephen) direct their creative efforts and find their completion.

The mystery of the Trinity is important in Joyce's esthetic, as Stephen indicates in "Scylla and Charybdis": "On that mystery and not on the madonna which the cunning Italian intellect flung to the mob of Europe the church is founded and founded irremovably because founded, like the world, macro- and microcosm, upon the void. Upon incertitude, upon unlikelihood" (*U* 207). This Catholic truism, dealing with the central mystery of faith, infinitely beyond the grasp of reason, forms the basic rock of Catholicism, and is unassailable by human or diabolic efforts to remove it. It will and must remain, to reason, both uncertain and unlikely, based in the void of unknowing available to faith but not to reason, nor to human experience as it is embodied in something as universal as the madonna and child. As Jackson Cope has perceptively pointed out, when Bloom feels the cold of interstellar space (*U* 704), he is feeling macrocosm.[7] Stephen can penetrate, in his own squidlike mission into the universe outside the human trinity within 7 Eccles Street, that limitless void, but Bloom turns back to the human warmth of female flesh. The incertitude with which Joyce fumbled in *Exiles* becomes the one base from which the artist, like the Catholic theologian, can operate. The theologian bases his assent on the act of faith in God's revelation; the artist bases his vision on the experience within him, also in purely rational terms uncertain and unlikely: "you have reared your disunited kingdom on the vacuum of your own most intensely doubtful soul" (*FW* 188). Justius the rational considers this offensive, as rationalists have found the Catholic faith, but Mercius seems to find his best defense in being founded, like the macro- and microcosm, upon that vacuum, that void of mystery.

The madonna is approached by Joyce in a way different from that which Stephen contemptuously assigns to the Vatican, a way which reflects Stephen's own adolescent reaction to devotion to Mary in *Portrait*.[8] The more sophisticated Stephen sees the Mariolatry in which he luxuriated as a lure, like that of the Temptress of the Villanelle, used by the cunning jesuitical hierarchy to trap the emotional and sentimental. Joyce had already portrayed, in the hazy story underlying the *Chamber Music* songs, the progress of a lonely sentimentalist through courting, union, and disillusion back to loneliness. A similar progress in *Dubliners,* as in "Araby" or the brutal female ruthlessness of "The Boarding House," indicates that Joyce had early recovered from at least the naïve extremes of romantic sentimentalism. In a funny and, at least for me, most subtle touch in *Ulysses,* Joyce illustrates the contrast between the madonna of Courtly Love and the Dublin woman cherished by twentieth-century poet-mystics. Bloom, tracking down a modest lunch, hears AE, "Beard and bicycle" (*U* 165), speaking to a young woman about a two-headed octopus, "one of whose heads is the head upon which the ends of the world have forgotten to come, while the other speaks with a Scotch accent." Bloom, who probably does recognize the quotation from Pater's *Renaissance* essay on Mona Lisa, guesses that the young woman might be the Lizzie Twigg he had remembered on *U* 160.[9] Bloom later recalls the sloppy stockings, when Stephen has mentioned Leonardo (*U* 637). Victory Pomeranz convincingly points out that Stephen most probably means Leonardo of Pisa,[10] a mathematical contemporary of Aquinas, but I take it that Bloom understands him (or as usually in that chapter, misunderstands him) to mean Leonardo da Vinci, since he immediately speaks of the rumpled stockings he saw on the putative Lizzie. At any rate, it hit me one day while I was re-creating Joyce's vision in my own imagination, as well as I could, that it was very funny that AE was speaking of Lisa to Lizzie, that the ideal woman of Pater's magnificent prose was contiguous with this loose-stockinged concocter of gooey verse, a sort of literary equivalent of Stephen's madonna-whore (and of Joyce's, as in "The Boarding House") construct, also like Bloom's consideration of Milly as watered-down Molly.

Dublin women, in general, tend to represent in Joyce's work the kind of descent from the ideal that we see in the fair damsel of "Two Gallants." Or worse, as in Stephen's association of women with bloodsucking bats. No. 27 of *Chamber Music* had established the image and the principle.

> Though I thy Mithridates were,
>   Framed to defy the poison-dart,
> Yet must thou fold me unaware
>   To know the rapture of thy heart,
> And I but render and confess
> The malice of thy tenderness.
>
> For elegant and antique phrase,
>   Dearest, my lips wax all too wise;
> Nor have I known a love whose praise
>   Our piping poets solemnize,
> Neither a love where may not be
>   Ever so little falsity.

Tindall notes the background of Housman's "Terence, this is stupid stuff" and thinks there is an allusion to his "sour attitude toward love." Maybe, but I do not find much sourness here. Joyce is, I suspect, thinking along the lines of the Herring *Ulysses Notesheets* notes for "Penelope," "fly-6 legs. spider-8" (p. 499) and "(female spider devours male after)" (p. 504). The speaker of the poem tells his dearest that she is an animal who, to fulfill her own nature (to know the rapture of her heart) must fold in her lover (and her prey). "Unaware" goes in two directions, expressing the lady's lack of awareness of her own animal selfishness, driving toward reproduction, and expressing also the necessity of keeping the prey unaware of his victim state, so that he will render himself up to "rendering" in all its varied senses, including butchery, and confess (go to confession, make known, admit not his own malice but, by submission, the malice inherent in her love). This is the temptress of the villanelle, based on the whore of chapter 2 of *Portrait* as well as on the madonna; most clearly Polly of "The Boarding House," revealed in the story's final sentence to be far more cold-blooded in her dealing with the victim even than her mother, the butcher's daughter; clearly enough handicapped Gertie, plotting ever more desperately to trap her man; obviously Molly, folding Bloom in her arms on Howth as she thinks "as well him as another"; even ALP, the most unselfish of all, as she neglects her husband for a time, not with the negligence of the combing Tennysonian woman of *CM,* No. 24, but in her concern for her dreaming and disturbed children.

The "elegant and antique" phrase might be "Love is not love which alters when it alteration finds," based as is that glorious Sonnet 116 of the greatest of English poets on the long tradition stemming from I Cor. 13, and the ideal unselfish love embodied in Christ's one commandment to his followers, "Love one another as I have loved you," which goes considerably beyond the old command to love the neighbor as yourself. Christ, after all, loved enough to give up his life for his friends. The speaker of the poem, changing like the moon but with Darwinian slowness, "waxes" too wise to accept the notion of totally unselfish love. Still, he does not dogmatize, but relies not on universal principle but on his own limited experience. He has not known a love like that which the young Shakespeare celebrated as the basis for literature and for the satisfactory completion of any man's being: "If this be error and upon me proved, I never writ, nor no man ever loved." Nor has he known the honest love that Hamlet, the pipe not easily played upon, demanded from Ophelia and from Gertrude, and judged that fraility could not live up to his ideal. The speaker of No. 27 is more modest, and accepts quite willingly his beloved with her modicum of falsity. Earlier drafts, which Tindall records in his edition, offer the feebly sentimental conclusion "But this I know—it scarce could be Dearer than is thy falsity." The published version is obviously stronger, and lends itself more obviously to the tendency to generalize.

Shakespeare's Sonnet 116 bases everything of value in literature and in life on the existence of unselfish love; Joyce's song doubts that a love without some touch of selfishness does or could exist. It does not preach a dogma, but just gives the speaker's experience and leaves the question of absolutely true love doubtful but open. It does not appear to me to be either cynical or sour, merely realistic. It operates along the line of Katharsis-Purgative of "The Holy Office," carrying off a touch of the filth cast by the pipers of dreamy dreams, but inoffensively. And, leaving aside the possibility of the operation of supernatural grace, it very likely accords with the experience of most or maybe of all young humans.

The speaker of *Chamber Music*, while he is too much occupied with his own thoughts and reactions and attitudes ("The Artist as an Adolescent"), sets before himself the goal of expressing the being of his beloved, her beauty and her love combined with her threat and her selfishness. As I can see Joyce's work, he himself worked in this fashion too, submitting himself to the good and the freedom of his characters, to express in the music of language their individual free choices and mysterious experience, and tending always to find the highest expression of the most important and basic aspects of human experience in a woman. This is clearly not true in *Portrait,* but if that is seen as a part of *Ulysses*, as it can be—or perhaps, as a novel which finds an unexpectedly sublime completion of itself in an even greater work—then it does not detract much, or any, from the principle I am trying to establish. Joyce is, of course, most immediately interested in himself as operating artist above all else, but that interest involves the thing with which his art most centrally concerns itself. Molly and ALP strike me as convincing demonstrations that the supreme concern of Joyce's art is with woman. Those critics who hold that *Ulysses* actually ends with the black dot at the end of "Ithaca" strike me as analogous to those who hold that human existence ceases with the last breath or the final heartbeat or with the cessation of brain waves. They leave out, I believe, all that our human experience prepares for. Everything in *Ulysses* prepares above all for what we find when we penetrate with Poldy (and with Joyce) that black dot, which I take to be (among the many things it can symbolize) Molly's anus, the lower portion of her proper 8, the entrance to those "bowels of misery" or "of mercy" from which the artist writes (Shem's necessary ink and artistic insight flows "through the bowels of his misery") and from which the woman's supreme love and yearning and human beauty spring.

I would have thought that final *Yes* which has been echoing through human imaginations since 1922 would have been one of the great expressions of human aspiration and frustration and completion and mystery, worthy to take its place with that most sublime of deathbed "lies," the "Nobody, I myself. Farewell" of Desdemona, or with the superhuman determination of "What should I stay—" of Cleopatra. And of course it is. But it can appear less cosmic only when it is set beside "A way a lone a last a loved a long the" of Anna Livia, where the "the" either links back with the first of the book's cosmic cycles or opens out into the infinite mystery upon which the eyes of prophets and poets from before our knowledge of human history have been fixed, seeking a "visible splendid sign." The definite article aims toward an existent, not an abstraction, and thus probes Being. And it may be an unfinished word, since it begins the Homeric name for god or goddess, *theos* or *thea,* which we would expect, even through the exercise of limited reason, to be unfinished in a human document, especially in one titled *Wake,* an end and a beginning. And in the expression of the most unselfish but also the most completely human woman of Joyce's (and maybe of any artist's) women, that small vocable becomes a cosmic portal of discovery.

In the opening lines of *Dubliners,* which begins with an echo of Dante's inscription over the entrance to hell, the boy dwells on words which in his ears sound "strange," the word Hippolyta used to describe Bottom's dream (or, more accurately, the lovers' account of events "more strange than true"). One of these is "gnomon" as he ran across it in his Euclid, a word which refers in geometry to an incomplete figure, and is thus useful for a frustrated and deformed world, like the stifling ignorance and paralysis and death in "The Sisters." The word also refers to secret religious knowledge, which is in a way the source of the priest's madness, as he sits in the confession box, where the "power" for which he had bartered his soul (as Stephen sees it, and Stephen Hero) presses in upon him as he sat "by himself in the dark in his confession-box," feeling like James Duffy the solipsism of hell, meeting the horror of his own human experience with mad soft laughter.

The voiceless sound merges with the irrational number in *Portrait,* as Stephen and his high-school fellows ponder the surd at the opening of chapter 3. There Stephen's imagination expands his equation into a cosmic peacock's tail, but for him the Christian symbol of resurrection indicates a weary cycle of frustration, expressed, like Gabriel Conroy's Shelleyan effort to fix in a phrase his reaction to his listening wife, as "a distant music" (*D* 228, *P* 354). His soul, echoing Father Flynn and James Duffy, folds back upon itself "fading slowly, quenching its own lights and fires," smothered in the cold darkness of chaos.

The dealing with Euclid perseveres into the core of *Finnegans Wake,* where "me elementator joyclid, son of a Butt" (*FW* 302) finds in the first Euclidean exercise, which produces a centrally significant equilateral triangle, one of the answers to the first riddle of the universe. For Shem the problem focuses upon what is for Shem (and no doubt for Joyce) the most interesting, the most obscene, and at the same time the most sacred area (as Catholics stress in the Hail Mary, "blessed is the fruit of thy womb") in the material universe—the sexual area of the female human being. As the two circles form themselves in relation to the straight line, in the figure on *FW*

293, Shem like the young Stephen sees symbolic levels, except that Shem's imagination projects him outside himself into the Other (or perhaps, since as Hart points out Shem is on *FW* 300 the Other, the irrational surd, and rational Shaun is the Same, it might be better to see Shem here too seeking his completion in the feminine Same). Shem sees those circles, as Bloom would, as the outlines of the bottom of Venus Kallipyge (as Buck calls the area of the goddess, woman as "life of life," to whom, as he says on *U* 201, we must all do daily homage, as he observed Bloom doing—Bloom, who plans that homage on *U* 176, in terms of "curves the world admires," would prefer, like the Joyce who urged Nora to drink cream and cocoa, Venus Steatopyge). Within the circles Shem watches the pubic delta form, with its mirror image dotted below it. And those circles, turning about in the fashion so brilliantly discussed by Clive Hart, form themselves not only into the infinity symbol but into the 8 which gives cosmic solidity to the significance of Molly Bloom.

It was the study of those circles, by the way, together with the combinations of 4s and 8s in the structuring of *FW*, that led me to look back at the operation of the 8 in "Penelope." I did not see any significance in all those 8s when I looked directly at the chapter before brooding over *FW*, and before seeing the amazing potentialities, beautifully explicated by Clive Hart in *Structure and Motif*, of those cycling circles symbolic both of the bottom of ALP and of the two sons expressive of aspects of their mother. Then my eyes began to be opened to the 8s of "Penelope," in relation to the "bottom" as one of Molly's key words, and in relation to her infinity and timelessness, and in relation to her 8 sentences (which surely became more and more significant to Joyce as he worked away from that loose "eight or nine sentences" concept with which he began [*Letters*, I: 168]).

Throughout the final chapter of *Ulysses*, the figure 8 shows up fifteen times, if my fading eyesight does not fail me.[11] The first two uses, in relation to the 8 roses Bloom gave to Molly on her birthday, September 8, grown out of an experience which I project into the imagination of the youthful Joyce comtemplating his first Euclidean (or Joyclidean) exercise, and watching those circles turn into the 8 of the birthday of the Blessed Virgin, whose knight I presume that he, like the overly fervent Stephen, wanted to be. (My projection is suggested to me by Stephen's seeing his equation turning like "The vast cycle of starry life" and sharing Gabriel's concern with "a distant music"—*P* 354.) Then I imagine that, like the equally lustful Stephen, he found the circles revealing themselves to him as those "moving hams" Bloom longed to see (*U* 59), and which Stephen, as I imagine, combined with the whores, arrayed for ritual around an altar (*P* 352, background for the villanelle), and the Virgin (*P* 357), where Stephen's twisted shy soul murmurs Mary's names with lips savoring lewd kisses (a foreshadowing of the nightly homage of Bloom). Thus I imagine Molly, as the ideal woman, early springing from goddess-madonna-whore experiences which the young Joyce, as I imagine him, projected into the circles of that figure which becomes so important in his climactic epic.

That "copious easychair," by the way, that Stephen noted in the whore's room, with the huge doll with her legs apart, haunted the ample erotic maze of Joyce's brain, apparently, since it has obvious connections with the "squat stuffed easychair with stout arms extended" in the Blooms' parlor. Hugh Kenner has recently focused our attention, in humorous and insightful speculation, on that chair and its "centralised diffusing and diminishing discolouration" (*U* 706).[12] Blazes had been seated in it, and the partly clothed Molly had sat on his knee, and we are left, like Kenner, to deduce from the violence to the rug and the stain on the chair's ample bottom what may have happened. One flaw in Kenner's reconstruction is his taking as reliable Molly's judgments on Mrs. Fleming. Molly seems rather kindly in excusing Mrs. Fleming's deficiencies on the basis of advanced age, but Molly considers thirty-five the terminal age for a woman, and she adds years to everyone's age except her own. Mrs. Rubio is eighty or a hundred, Bloom is advanced two years to forty, and even Stephen gets one or two years added on. For herself, she reluctantly accepts the fact that she has passed thirty and thinks of herself as thirty-one, then pretends some confusion and decides that she must be thirty-two since she will in three months be thirty-three, and she well knows all the time that she is thirty-three at the present moment. I myself guess that Mrs. Fleming is a husky fifty and together with Molly could move more pianos and sideboards than two Boylans could. And it strikes me too that the fussy Molly, having elaborately prepared herself for her maiden venture into adultery, would be acting out of accord with her conventional attitudes if she put husbandly or cleaning duties upon her lustful lover. Had she done so, it would have been a decision unusual enough to attract her attention in her nocturnal musings, and it would not have involved the grief or guilt that would cause her to repress it, as she does deliberately repress painful thoughts of Rudy. So I speculate that Molly and Mrs. Fleming moved both the piano and the sideboard, changing the setting before the Dublin Don Juan strutted onstage.

Like the circles, I take the two eggs which Molly mentions in her opening words, developing from the roc's egg of the previous page, to symbolize also Molly's 8, her genital area. One of the things the black dot which closes "Ithaca" symbolizes is that magic legendary egg which Sinbad saw and which Bloom in his conquering descent into the dark of his own being manages to square. There is an egg in Molly, and the huge roc which would properly have laid its egg on the Rock, birthplace of Molly, suggests Molly the Earth goddess metaphorically circling the sun, and the common auk which might have laid its egg on Howth could well suggest the real Molly who found conception there. The square around the egg suggests to me that 4 is the number assigned to Bloom, not the 8 which would make it possible for him to enter into full union with Molly. In her seventh sentence Molly complains of Bloom's big square feet up in her mouth, and reviews their 4 houses, Bloom's ineffectual help in moving their 4 sticks of furniture, and Bloom's 4 jobs. In her eighth and last sentence, she stresses again the 16 years they have been together, and in the first 16 words of that sentence (*U* 776), which deal with Boylan, there are 8 negatives. It appears, in the code I fancy I perceive throughout the patterning of 8s and 4s and 16s in this eighteenth chapter, that the 8 of Molly's mesial groove (two of the "Three holes all women" that Bloom speaks of on *U* 285) which has been fully usurped by Boylan, is here denied him. Thus in the last 16 words, which deal with Mulvey-Bloom, one might expect, if one thought that Bloom might regain the full husbandly rights and privileges which have been half denied to him, the satisfactory square of 4 yeses.

Joyce like Marianne Moore liked such coding and counting and patterning, and in the eight sentences of Molly's monologue I believe that I find another symbol of the two circles, in that the first four sentences stress the mature Molly and the second four stress the young Gibraltar Molly. The first sentence (738–44) deals with Molly's present and past dealings with Bloom; the fifth sentence (759–63) deals with the fifteen-year-old Molly's dealings with her first lover, Mulvey. Both deal with Molly as Calypso. Her second sentence (744–53) deals with the men Molly has encountered; her sixth sentence (763–70) deals with Gibraltar, with fifteen-year-old Molly, and in expanding imagery of mountains and giants and sea, concludes with Molly making a huge row on the pot while she repeats with a suggestive change Southey's "How does the water come down at Lodore," a nursery poem. Her short third sentence (753–54) deals passionately with her adultery; her seventh sentence (770–76) begins with the young Molly's being courted by Bloom and ends with the possibility of an affair with the young Stephen. Her fourth sentence (754–59) begins with the strength of men and ends with the weakness of women, dealing in its central portion with the young Molly's Gibraltar friend, Hester Stanhope; her eighth sentence (776–83) begins with the crudity of Boylan and winds its way through to the mingling of the young and mature Molly with Mulvey and Bloom on Gibraltar and Howth, all mixing in time and space as Molly herself, like Bloom before her, slips into the Real Absence (*FW* 536) of her ink.

Whether or not Molly is a loving woman, ultimately, I do not know, nor, as I can understand the matter, did Joyce. He loved her, I am sure, as he loved Nora, and as Shem really loved his unchanging sacred Word in the way Shaun, probably hypocritically, claims to: "The word is my Wife, to expanse and expound, to vend and to velnerate, and may the curlews crown our nuptias! Till Breath us depart! Wamen" (*FW* 167). And he accepts Molly as she is, without question and without desire to have her more perfect or less limited. He does not, to my mind, exhibit at all what Ellmann, in the concluding lines of *Ulysses on the Liffey*, thinks that he sees, "a certain embarrassment and reticence. He speaks of love without naming it." Joyce does not speak of love. He does create a woman who may or may not be ultimately loving. He does not attempt to pry into that mystery because he well knows what every true artist knows and what every Catholic should know, that only God can know and judge that ultimate hidden choice of the free human spirit. The Joyce who created Molly was probably more aware than was the speaker of *Chamber Music* that there might be a love without falsity, but in neither case did he speak didactically, nor did he fear that he might do so. If he could know whether it was ultimately there or not, he would have no hesitation in naming it. But he cannot know, and he knows he cannot, and he accepts that ultimate mystery. He does know perfectly well that the act of adultery is not necessarily an act of rejection of Bloom. It may even be an effort to come nearer to him, unlikely as that seems. But Joyce doesn't name love because he does not know whether Molly loves or not; Bloom doesn't know, Molly herself doesn't know, and therefore it ought to be clear that we are not going to know. God may know, but if so, as Elijah informs us in "Circe," "he ain't saying nothing" (*U* 508).

With the motion of the river rushing into the ocean, Joyce expresses the ultimate in his vision of woman in the perfect closing pages of *Finnegans Wake,* and more than Hamlet remembered the ghost who called to him, we who have heard the dying and waking voice of Anna will remember her. There is nothing in literature to surpass the moving music of these pages, and they give all the assurance we will ever get that Stephen's feet did scale Tara.

3 "A fortifine popespriestpower bull of attender to booth"

Happily, we can determine exactly where the Joycean sacrament of penance begins. Joyce carries it back beyond Christ into a quotation from David translated into Latin (Ps. 74:10, King James 75:10), involving a pun on lifted horns and erect penises: "*Et exaltabuntur cornua justi*. Queens lay with prize bulls. Remember Pasiphae for whose lust my grandoldgrossfather made the first confessionbox" (*U* 569). It is Stephen's pun, less obviously gross than those of Mulligan and Lenehan, but more profound and bitterly condemnatory than theirs, too. The horns are those of bulls, fat bulls of Bashan, perhaps, from Ps. 21:13, chanted liturgically in the Tenebrae service of Holy Week, which Joyce attended throughout his life. The horns no doubt spring also from that papal and English bull so vividly allegorized by Dixon, Vincent, and Stephen (*U* 399–401). The bull in Stephen's mind here is that magnificent white bull which Minos, perhaps with a predilection for handsome white bulls owing to his own paternity, had kept back from sacrifice, and which thus fathered that mixed monster, the Minotaur, which was Stephen's central image for himself as he wandered the maze of Dublin seeking virgins. Bloom is, according to Dowie, the white bull of the Apocalypse (*U* 492), which in Dowie's mind must be some mixture of one or other of the apocalyptic beasts, which do not include bulls, with the Ovidian Jove who as a white bull together with Europa generated Minos, husband to Pasiphae. Pasiphae, in her turn, lusting after another white bull, in bestial subsubstantiation managed to conceive that Minotaur who served as an image of the beastly Stephen stalking virgins in the maze of Dublin. Panther-Bloom metamorphoses into many beasts in the "midsummer madness" (*U* 492) of

"Circe"—Bello even finds him a great source of milk. Among others he becomes an ass (*U* 496), perhaps in some way connected with the Eviction Act, but deriving from other sources also. Zoe has already nibbled on his ear (*U* 477), and when those ears become asses' ears a few pages later, we are in the mood to see Bottom, whose long pliant ears were fondled by Titania, even more than we are conditioned to recognize Midas. It is the "bare bot" of Bloom which Bello threatens (*U* 539). And of the careers open to the young Bloom, attractive is the art of the actor, tragic like the most famous Hamlet of the time, Osmond Tearle, or comic like the high comedian, Charles Wyndham (*U* 690), a fine background for producing a Woful Dane's Bottom. In such a context it seems to me more than likely that the final "Heighho" of St. George's message to Bloom is his summons to his Peter Quince, Stephen, to bang out a ballad of a Father and of a Gaseous Vertebrate, a gas-filled Molly, or of Titubante and his Anastashie—a ballad far more profound than the product of the perverse balladeer of Joking Jesus. Buck's poem celebrates the bringing forth of Jesus-Stephen-Joyce by a bird—the dove symbolizing the Holy Ghost, called "gaseous vertebrate" by Buck as he enters a discussion of the ghost of Hamlet's father and hears the other elements of the sign of the cross, father and son (*U* 197). Thus Buck dwells on Stephen as Jesus not in his divine nature eternally brought forth by the Father but as the man brought forth by Mary overshadowed by the Holy Ghost. That ballad, a contrast to the Quincian ballad desired by Bottom, can be seen as Buck's supreme effort, repeated like the Angelus many times a day at mealtime, to suppress and overwhelm and to abort the creations of Stephen. His attack on Bloom in the library and his warnings to Stephen to avoid with a breechpad Bloom's threat to attempt atonement with Stephen stem, I judge, from his intuition of the possibility that Bloom might actually bring Stephen into life-giving contact with the heaven-born earth. If Buck does want to keep Stephen as a catamite (*U* 204), as I think he does, and if as a dominating prelate he wants to prevent Stephen's art from revealing the hellish shallowness of his own Hellenism, then he might well fear that melon which the Eastern Man will offer to Stephen. And he may get some glimpse of Stephen's ingesting that human eucharist with his ears, with St. George's help, and with his eyes from the light glimmering through Molly's shade.

The ass in his vision on *FW* 404 knows as well as Puck does in the epilogue to *A Midsummer Night's Dream* that the "shadow" of literature is more real than the human beings who walk the streets of London or of Dublin. Puck speaks of Theseus-types, who are too rationalistic and unimaginative to perceive that he is really telling them that they are leaving the chaosmos which opens the bottom of reality when they wake up and achieve "full fost sleep" (*FW* 473). They leave the Globe or the ink of *FW*, where heaven and hell may be glimpsed, to return to the dull limits of their conscious reason. The stylish apparition who emerges on *FW* 404, whom we dreamt (in the various senses of "fancied," "intuited," "imagined," "contrived") was a shadow, is not only "lifesize" but brings light to the darkened eyes. And in looking at and listening to him we will see and know that we too are such stuff as dreams are made on, and, as Paul cried out to the blind and deaf Corinthians, we must share this most rare vision, this glimpse through the Spirit of God (or of the godlike artist), if we are to surpass (or sink beneath) the wisdom of this age or of the rulers of this age—rationalists like Theseus, for example. So the lecturer of *FW* 119 can say, in opposition to rationalists represented on that page by Wyndham Lewis ("this will never do"), that *Finnegans Wake* itself may be our only hope to survive the deluge—"cling to it as with drowning hands."

As it was Shakespeare who was the real Peter Quince—as well as the real Bottom and Titania, and all the others, "all in all"—still, he was Peter Quince in a special sense, as Shakespeare the actor playing his character of the elder Hamlet was in a duplicated sense the father of all his race. So it is Joyce who is the "poor ass" in a double sense, both as he is every one of his characters and as, in a special sense, he is the seer and expounder of the dream, the Bottom and the Peter Quince, as only the lord of the "nonland of where's please," one who can call all others, "you and they" (*FW* 403) to share in his own individual experience, to become through him "we."

The wife of King Minos, Pasiphae, was cursed by the angry Poseidon with a lust for that concealed bull, and she, in her need, did what Stephen did at the end of *Portrait*. She prayed for help to Daedalus, the old father, the artificer, the "altus prosator" of Shem (*FW* 185). Ovid relates her activity in the section of *Metamorphoses* immediately preceding the passage from which the epigraph of *Portrait* is taken. Daedalus, ever helpful, not in forging a conscience for his race but in assisting in advancing the bestial urges and in incarcerating the consequent monsters emanating from his employers, stood Pasiphae then if not ever in good stead by constructing for her a wooden cow in which, like the Greek heroes in the wooden horse, she could by deception triumph.

The bull, by the way, so pervasive in the confessional passages of Joyce's work—as when Butt mutters his "meac Coolp" "in open ordure" of the bullish "oneship" (*FW* 344), or when as "bullock" Yawn is offered the "moral turptitude" of "playing bull before shebears" (*FW* 522)—lies behind the confrontation of Stephen and Cranly with the old dwarf, Farrell, in *Portrait* (227–28).[1] Stephen, with his confessor, Cranly, who had perhaps been in some way preparing for Stephen's next confession in reading *Diseases of the Ox*, sees the old man as the diseased product of incest, a model like many of the *Dubliners* characters of the deterioration of the once-noble Irish. The dwarf's interest in Scott's melodramatic *The Bride of Lammermore* ties him both to the pervert of "An Encounter" and to Shaun (and HCE) as possibly allied to Ivanhoe's slave Gurth, in the name "Gugurtha" (*FW* 403), with perhaps the moral decay revealed in Scott's degraded style and the remnants of British idealism clinging to Gurth both involved. At any rate, Stephen seems to be brooding on the evils of an autocratic, king-ridden state, the companion of a sinister, priest-ridden church. He must fight against them, like a noble, lonely, antlered elk, or, it may be, in this Clontarfian area, a powerful bull. He is thus more like Davin than Cranly, and it is the hands of Davin that appear in his sexual fantasy of the ancestors of Farrell stealthily embracing in the garden. His own father's gibes at the Bantry gang, enemies of Parnell, sound in his ears and, like a beleagured animal, "he held them at a distance." I suspect that he has also reluctantly realized that he is like that powerful bull which charged the noble Lord of Lammermore and his daughter, and that he sees old Farrell as a Dublin Master of Ravenswood who killed the bull in the nick of time. Thus the proud Stephen, forging a conscience for his race, can be brought down in a moment by the gentle movement of the dwarf's thin shrunken brown hand.

In any case, the Stephen of "Circe" pictures that wooden structure into which Pasiphae crept to achieve union with another bull as "the first confessionbox." I remember the shock and puzzlement with which I first encountered that image, no doubt because I do not, like Stephen, tend to see Catholic attitudes and practices as intrinsically evil and perverse. Therefore that construct of Stephen's struck me as a vast leap from something bestial and unnatural to an effort to denigrate something in itself sacred and beautiful. While I had shared a good deal of Stephen's tortuous experience with the confession box, I also knew, as he did, that Catholicism regards the box as a means for reestablishing divine love and union; I cannot remember, however, quite the extremes of that "white rose" imagery of Stephen after his own sly effort to bring God to terms in his own confession. That basic hypocrisy is, at least, what I see in Stephen's effort to fulfill what he understood to be the terms of the sacrament. Like Hopkins in "My own heart," Stephen wanted to wring God's smile from Him, through a mechanical and profitable cash register procedure, in which he would submit and perform acts of charity, and God would reward him with happiness and salvation.

After a good deal of reflection, however, I came to perceive some good solid reasons for Stephen's image, and to realize also that his response to the sacrament was not altogether different from mine, in spite of the bitter disillusion to which he came. He had very early, in his own fantasizing about being a priest, considered the pleasures of hearing the secret sins of girls whispered through the lattice. These thoughts merged easily both with the foul notes he deposited in odd corners where girls might find them and with the Catholic attitude that in the confessional he—or, he might put it, his shy and sinful female soul—could return to the intimate loving relationship with God which is the completion of human nature, in the Catholic view. Stephen was not unaware of Catholic attitude, and as I see the matter he was not unaware either that his "Circe" cynicism about the confession box flowed at least as much from his own response as from the nature of the box itself. He left that matter open, and though, as he says about human love in *CM*, No. 27, he had himself never known an act of totally unselfish love—none that he could absolutely identify as such—still, he does not dogmatically assert, like Ayn Rand, for example, that no one else has ever known one either, though he clearly suspects that such might be the case. I speak of Stephen, a young man.

Thus the mixture of abuse of human love through bestial sexual union, particularly when the beast involved at least shared in the aura of the Greek notions of divinity, could quite easily lead Stephen to see Daedalus's structure as a confession box. I had early on in my musings on the image considered Stephen's probable view of Daedalus as a careful carpenter, like Jesus, forming a cow—an image for Ireland ("milk of the kine") and for the Church, as a source of the life-giving milk in the land of milk and honey, even at times, as in Hopkins's image of the Church as cow,[2] a source of grace—like that moo cow, symbolic of Ireland, the Church, and woman, who wanders into literature in the opening words of *Portrait*. The stealthy entry of Pasiphae into the narrow wooden structure then came to seem not altogether alien to Stephen's view of E. C. entering the box to whisper into Father Moran's "latticed ear." Molly, too, a few pages after Stephen's image of Pasiphae united to the bull, will admire the bullneck of her confessor seen through the lattice. Gradually I came to perceive something of the connection Stephen saw between the lusts these Catholic women carried into the box and the lust the sister of Circe took into her cow.

Joyce is also preparing for his treatment of Molly as the Holy Spirit, that invisible Third Person of the Trinity, to be symbolized in the glowing light from Molly's bedchamber: "How did he elucidate the mystery of an invisible person, his wife Marion (Molly) Bloom, denoted by a visible splendid sign, a lamp?" (*U* 702). In "The Sisters," there is indication that following the madness and death of the priest, the ignorant old ladies, foreshadowing the senile he-ladies Mamalujo of *FW*, take over the management of the Church and the sacraments, at least the Eucharist. Here in "Circe" Joyce "ordains" the woman Pasiphae, who must operate as priest as well as penitent, allied by geographical ties to the Molly born on, or near, Europa Point (Europa was Pasiphae's mother-in-law), and sister of the Homeric enchantress Circe, so similar to Calypso-Molly, the fortune-teller and enslaver of men. Pasiphae, in the first confession box, becomes the first confessor, and thus, as we see Anna Livia at the end of chapter 7 absolving both Confessor-Justius and Confessee-Mercius, we discover that priestly power too, like life and love, in Joyce's vision proceeds from woman.

I stress that the profundity and much of the power of Joyce's confession-box image derives, at least for me, from the positive Catholic view, which Stephen is bitterly questioning, that the confession box is a love box, in which the priest, an alter-Christus, serves as a mediator between a human sinner and the infinitely loving Trinity. Joyce well understood the demands exerted upon human nature by this power of the priest, so frenetically celebrated by the spiritual director in *Portrait,* and as Stephen had thought of the effect on Simon Magus as he listened to the director, so the young narrator of the first of the *Dubliners* stories thinks of simony in a story which ends in madness in a confession box. Even more pointedly that box appears in a more powerful story, "A Painful Case," where Duffy perverts the sacrament to his own ends in Mrs. Sinico's living room. He wanted to use it to effect her adoration of him, as there he ascended "to an angelical stature," preaching the dogma dear to Ayn Rand and to Milton's Satan, that "we are our own," *non serviamus.* But Mrs. Sinico, like Sybil Vane offering to Dorian Gray her simple human love instead of her artistic portrayal of an ideal, literary love, destroyed everything by treating that inverted aged Dublin "artist" as if he were an ordinary human. Duffy meets her away from "the influence of their ruined confessional" to break things off, and thus avoids even a chance of human love involving him in a relationship with another. As he stands in the darkened park, further darkening "venal loves," the train which had killed Mrs. Sinico winds through the dark like the fiery-headed worm of hell, which Christ had said would not die and which, in the Retreat in *Portrait,* will eat into the eye of the damned.[3] Duffy realizes the Catholic insight into hell when he feels that he is alone.

The pressure on a real priest who apparently does want to exercise fully the priestly power seems to me the focus of "The Sisters." Father Flynn has failed in his effort to raise the chalice, one of his central functions, but behind that failure is a deeper one, his failure to keep himself, as a mediator between a human person and God, uninvolved in the confessional—"uninvolved" in the sense of not supposing that he himself is the ultimate source of the forgiveness accorded. As I can understand the matter, one source of Father Flynn's own inner tension may have been a failure to face and with humility accept and endure and repent of his own sinfulness. A shadowy insight into this situation by the boy helps to explain that dream of the reversed roles. That dream, by the way, foreshadows *FW,* in its moving below the conscious operation of the mind to probe the deeper mysteries of human experience. In the boy's perceptive dream, the old priest comes vacuously smiling to the boy's latticed ear, in the pleasant vicious region which he was unwilling or unable to acknowledge as existing within him, and which he was too human or too honest, it may be, to suppress without paralyzing injury to his reason. The confession box is a dangerous place for humans, the story indicates, as Father Flynn returns to the spot where he was supposed to bring together sinful humans and the infinite God, and, sitting in the backwash of his own frustrated nature, laughs softly to himself. Since Father Flynn is the central priest of the three in the chapel,[4] he readily symbolizes the Second Person, the

Word rendered speechless,[5] paralyzed by his own bartering of his human lusts and loves for the power of managing those of other humans. This is his crime, his selling in simoniac exchange his freedom for power over others, and it is their crime if, like Stephen in superstitious bargaining hypocrisy, they lay their sins on his back. He is thus a symbol of Catholic Ireland, as was the Ireland Joyce saw as the object of Mangan's worship: "In the final view the figure which he worships is seen to be an abject queen upon whom, because of the bloody crimes that she has done and of those as bloody that were done to her, madness is come and death is coming."[6]

This view, it seems to me, bolsters the valuable studies of Florence Walzl, whose insight into the G.P.I. of Father Flynn illuminates both the story and Joyce's vision of the matter. Flynn's disease may stem from actual syphilis, but it may also, and more likely does, stem from metaphorical spiritual syphilis, an infection from a Church guilty of fornication with a rotten State. But for that opening story of *Dubliners,* a principal stone in the structure of penance imagery, the center of infection for Father Flynn, as his sterile old sisters also know, is the abused confession box.

Five confessions centering in sexual involvement will indicate how individuals, society, religion, the lustful, and the relatively healthy make use of that box. It is a metaphorical box in the first instance, but one which, as I can see the matter, does fit into and furnishes a base for the succeeding use of real boxes. *CM,* No. 27, no doubt under the influence of Housman, portrays the young lover "framed" in a double or triple sense against the "poison-dart" of female love. The mood, I believe, is one influenced by such broodings as those which produced the note in the "Penelope" notesheets—"crim. spider—idiot oldest insect fly-6 legs. spider-8"[7] "(female spider devours male after)"[8]—and which sees all the Gracehoper's friends as biting or stinging insects, "Floh and Luse and Bienie and Vespatilla" (*FW* 414). The tenderness of the woman involves her own selfish natural needs, at the very least, with perhaps a personal dash of malice spicing the mixture. And he, the somewhat limp and endangered male, can only "render and confess." A rendering process is, in some of its aspects, a weakening one, and a confession like this one—the rhetoric and rhythm suggest that it is wrung from him—reveals an elegant, gilded-age, lily-fingering surrender on the part of the speaker. It goes well with Stephen's villanelle, a stronger poem, in which the speaker realizes the enervating effect of the luring he will not resist. There it is the black mass which gives depth, and here in *CM,* No. 27, I seem to detect the confession box looming behind that "confess." James Duffy—and as one learns to look for Shakespeare in his "wills in surplus" one looks for Joyce in his numerous Jameses—wished to "render" Mrs. Sinico, in the sense of draining the independent personality out of her, in his inverted confessing. Shem, in the confession in chapter 7 of *FW* which I see as the climax of Joyce's use of this image, "renders" himself to the untender pontifical bull which overlays Justius's imperious bill of attainder, and finds himself caught up and absolved by his mother. In *CM*, No. 27, the very young speaker "renders" himself with some kind of fascinated and masochistic delight in being violated, a situation which the young Stephen encounters with the young whore in *Portrait*, which Richard displays in *Exiles*, and which Bloom enacts in "Circe." This kind of "con-fession" or speaking-with has a connection, I believe, with the kind of "con-science" or knowing-with which the artist as young man intends to forge for his race.

I suspect that Joyce learned a meaning of "conscience" from Bishop Trench's *On the Study of Words*: "Again, here is conscience, a solemn word, if there be such in the world. There is not one of us whose Latin will not bring him so far as to tell him that this is from con and scio. But what does that con intend? . . . The word in fact grows out of and declares that awful duplicity of our moral being which arises from the presence of God in the soul" (pp. 234–35). Joyce, with his image of the artist as God the Creator in mind, would have had no difficulty at all in adapting these words to his (and Stephen's) purpose. When Stephen speaks of forging the uncreated conscience of his race, he is probably thinking of the duplicity he as creative artist intends to create in the individuals of his race, a duplicity which will arise not from the presence of God but from the presence of the artist in the reader's soul. Instead of knowing-with God, Stephen's readers will know-with Stephen the godlike artist, forming his verbal cosmos (or chaosmos) in their souls as, reading the "black ink," they form their own words in their imaginations.

This "conscience" of which Stephen speaks is less a moral urge than a revelatory urge, less movement to some end than an apprehension of a mysterious and relatively timeless present moment that the young artist aims at in his forging. At any rate, in the mind of the speaker of *CM*, No. 27, every male in his situation ought to examine whether he has ever known, as the speaker has not, a love like that celebrated by Shakespeare in Sonnet 116 or by St. Paul in 1 Cor. 13, both of them, for this most superior young man, "piping poets." And if the reader (or better, hearer) has not, then he ought to join this speaker in the confession which involves both sorrow and joy, both hate and love, both hell and heaven.

The confession of Bob Doran in "The Boarding House" may be taken as an example of the domestic or society-pressured confession, allied in some ways to the confession of May Dedalus so offensive to Stephen Hero. In an echo of the "render" of the poem, "the priest had drawn out every ridiculous detail" from the unhappy Doran, "rendering" this lamb for Mrs. Mooney's efficient sacrifice, and Polly's even more destructive and deadly one. It caused Bob "acute pain," and it beautifully illustrates one function of the confession box in a society where some remnants of a medieval "sense of honour," rather soiled as in "Two Gallants," can be focused to bring pressure simultaneously from Church and State. The success of the sacrificial liturgy of the butcher's daughter can be gauged by her final sentence, "Mr. Doran wants to speak to you," his own final and fatal rendering and con-fessing.

Stephen's own climactic confession at the end of chapter 3 of *Portrait,* on the surface comparable to The Croppy Boy's honest confession in "Sirens" of *Ulysses,* has seemed to many the act of a good Catholic. Mr. Tindall opined at one time that if the book had ended at that point, Catholics would have praised it as a revelation of the truth and beauty of the only true religion.[9] He may have been right, but if so those Catholics would have been even more ignorant and perverse in their praise than in their actual condemnation. And even had he been right when he said it, he would not be right in saying it now, because one Catholic at least sees Stephen's confession as a far more devilish act than his fornication. Stephen himself stresses that the quality of the act of confession, lost in the profound depths of the inviolable psyche, cannot be judged except in the light of consequences. Stephen emerges from his confession box filled with romantic lush images and moronic sentence structures, and not Christ but the ciborium comes to him. His mechanical schemes for acquiring virtue in terms of cash on the line and his increasing withdrawal from the condemnation of his family and friends reveal gradually to his own observant intellect how false is this formal pretense of love. Finally his artistic but impersonal involvement with the bird-girl in the water he would himself not enter and his final resolve to buckle on the Icarian wings and wing away on his wild-goup's chase across the kathartic ocean demonstrate his flight from that box which he found to be not a channel to divine love but a profoundly obscene coalhole.

Gerty MacDowell, in the context of that real man of whom she constantly dreamed, crushing her soft body to him and loving her, his ownest girlie, for herself alone, allows her lustful musings to slide through the praises of the all-powerful sorrowing Virgin to the hands, "just like white wax" (*U* 358), of Father Conroy, whom Bloom thinks (*U* 377), probably mistakenly, to be the brother of Gabriel, whose mother disapproved of Gretta.[10] Gerty imagined Father Conroy helping at the altar, carrying things in and out with his eyes cast down. In his confession box, "so quiet and clean and dark," a fine and private place, she confessed, apparently, that she had begun to menstruate— like Molly, Gerty cuts her age back as many years as she can manage—and he took quite a bit of time to assure her of the fact that Molly could compress into two words, "only natural." He urged her to consider her likeness to Our Blessed Lady, but his picturing Mary in colloquy with the archangel Gabriel rather tends, at least in the crimson lust of Gerty's mind, to transform his confessional into a virgin's chamber. The ruched "teacosy" she thought he might like, appropriate in the tea-eucharist symbolism of the book, would be covered with her embroidered flowers, perhaps roses like those Molly wants all around her. Or a clock, though their clock with a canary bird already tells him the time, which will soon for Gertie be too short for gathering rosebuds for forty hours or years. These confessional images with their flora and fauna content link Gertie to the whores in Bella's house, Flossie and Kitty, and her album of illuminated views of Dublin or some place suggest Zoe with her negation of life. That someplace, to which Father Conroy's box can offer entrance to Gertie, is not heaven.

Unlike Gerty in this as in many things, Molly hates "that confession" (*U* 741). And Molly's approach to Father Corrigan's hand contrasts with Gerty's hypocritical admiration for a waxen saintly image. Like the Mae West of the thirties bringing the fresh air of unveiled lust into the fetid pretense of the coy sex movies popular then, Molly admires that "nice fat hand the palm moist always I wouldn't mind feeling it" on the bottom about which the confessor was inquiring with the indirection that stirred honest Molly's impatience. Molly's bottom at least was honest, in the background of Joyce's "Ithaca" note, "(Woman's arse honest),"[11] which may be why Bloom sought his comfort there rather than in the Greek mouth never twisted in prayer which Mulligan claimed to prefer (*U* 201). Molly longs to be embraced by a priest in his vestments, and in the context of her having bared an ankle to keep Bloom in his new raincoat—the "pluviale" of the priestly Shem (*FW* 185) was a raincoat for the ancient Romans, a cope or chausable for the current Vatican ones—from kneeling in the rain, it is too bad that, as she smells the incense Bloom had lighted in the adjoining room, she does not realize that the kiss of peace of the black mass has been liturgically bestowed upon her honest natural arse.

Molly's confession is the only one that does not cause pain or perversion, and, outside of the mild annoyance at the priest's casuistical questioning, she enjoyed it enough to get Father Corrigan's name on the list of admirers the Odyssean Bloom, returned to his rightful if deceptive bed—from old Cohen's rather than, as Molly had told Bloom, from Gibraltar[12]—had to destroy with indifference. But though it did Molly no harm, it did her no perceptible good either.

The ultimate confession in the series that Joyce employs is that to which Shem is summoned by his priestly brother on page 188 of *FW*. Claiming to know all the shames of this son of Adam, Shaun as judging Justius assures Shem that he will need not only the waters of the Jordan but that priestly power so much impressed on the schoolboy Stephen by the spiritual director, and even the highest operation of that power in the Supreme Priest's bull attending to deal with Shem's monstrous crimes.

The long examination of conscience uncovers as the first crime that Shem builds his world, not on God's revelation as brought to him by the Church, but "on the vacuum of your own most intensely doubtful soul." All of his other sins follow from this original sin, his sexual misdeeds, his seeking out the evil in a good word (as in finding "ever so little falsity" in all human love in *CM*, No. 27). As an artist, as *FW* 190-91 set forth, he imitated Oscar Wilde in becoming at least a literary sodomite ("a thoroughpaste prosodite"), dealing with cheeks of language as Shakespeare ("Scheekspair"), according to Oscar Wilde's fictional construct in *The Portrait of Mr W H,* dealt with the cheeks of Willie Hughes (the W. H. so prominent on many pages of *FW*). But most of all (or perhaps it is merely the climax of his literary crimes), he smote, like a murderous Cain, his "ittle earps brupper" and laid him low. Justius offers him medicine for "the solitary worm," recalling both Stephen's attitude toward his rebellious penis[13] and James Duffy's feeling himself alone. Justius invites Shem to look in the glass and see the madman who will not serve, and in his liturgical nonabsolution he lifts one of the bones making up the cross of the two thieves on the Tunc page of the *Book of Kells,* reproduced on *FW* 308, the bone of the *Dio Boia* that crushes the self into submission.

Shem as Mercius actually does confess, and acknowledges the charges of Justius. He admits, with a confusion of pronouns, that he has violated his union with his brother, that he has tried to dominate his doom—the passage in parentheses indicates that his father's experience on *FW* 30–31, which is also his own experience, is still going on and will go on to doomsday, do what he sinfully will to extricate himself from it—and he sees himself as Bully Bottom, Nick the clown-artist, lying on the bank of secret human longings where Thyme is overcome by Woman, the ass embraced by the fairy queen, man atoned with God. "Astroglodynamonologos," the word for the artist, stems from Theseus' condemnation of the poet,[14] who in the service of Imagination glances from the stars to the troglodytic holes, with dynamic and lonely power bringing forth the *logos*. And the goddess Imagination as ALP flows into his confession and brings the brothers together as she both de-Luthers[15] and Luthers the sacrament, making all one in the "only natural," so that Shem, absolved, can lift the other element of the cross, the kiss, the X of mystery, and as a refrillfrocked quackfriar, sound his wild-goose call to life across the void.

Thus the two elements in the confessional, the death of sin and the life of love, symbolized by the bones, come together in the loving and hating cross which is the woman's "criss-cross" at the end of the Letter, and which finds its fullest expression in *FW*'s chapter 8 and in the sublime music of the book's concluding pages. Joyce will accept things the way they are, but, as his Catholic experience early informed him, in its acceptance of strict mystery, he does not know how they ultimately are. What he does know is that along with the falsity and pain, there are also exciting beauty and pleasure, and his confession box is open to both aspects. I suppose each of us will respond more to the aspect which most appeals to us and which we are prepared to perceive. Everyone sees Joyce's vision as a catholic one, and from my own angle, at least, I can see it also as a Catholic one.

4 Joyce's Esthetic

> if one has the stomach to add the breakages, upheavals distortions, inversions of all this chambermade music one stands, given a grain of goodwill, a fair chance of actually seeing the whirling dervish, Tumult, son of Thunder, self exiled in upon his ego—*Finnegans Wake* (184)

Gerard Hopkins, in April of 1879, having returned as a priest to the Oxford he had entered and loved some fifteen years earlier, had renewed his contact with Pater and had revived, like the Oscar Wilde who so deeply influences the quotation above, the Paterian drive to value the reactions of the self even more than the clear burning of a candle in night's blear-all black or a new-forged bright and battering sandal. Then of the chambermade music of Purcell, Hopkins wrote

> It is the forgèd feature finds me; it is the rehearsal
> Of own, of abrúpt sélf there so thrusts on, so throngs the ear.

The unique feature of the individual person, forged in the smithy of the soul, as Ben Jonson saw the lines of Shakespeare forged to reflect the very mind and manners of their "father," comes into new being in the seeing hearer. Hopkins in "As kingfishers" states more clearly the activity of the self—

> Each mortal thing does one thing and the same:
> Deals out that being indoors each one dwells;
> Selves—goes itself; *myself* it speaks and spells,
> Crying *What I do is me: for that I came.*

Hopkins is paraphrasing the words of Christ before Pilate, "for this have I come into the world" (John 18:37), of Truth expressing the true. Pilate, as Hopkins saw it (and as Joyce at least at one time did), was being given an opportunity of actually seeing God in the self before him; Christ was dealing out divine being in his speaking and spelling.

In all his own chambermade music, Joyce like Christ "plays in ten thousand places," sounding out on his magic Jew's harp a whirling self as noisy in our streets as was that fiercely verbal John whom Christ named "Son of Thunder." Like the angels, at least those who followed the "Catholic" translation—"good will to men" was "Protestant," like "debts" instead of "trespasses" in the Our Father—of the Bethlehem song, Joyce seeks the ears of "men of goodwill," that, hearing, they might see not merely a page of coded ink (merely a human babe in a manger) but the dynamically operating self of a human being (the finite "modality" of infinite Being). More than Pater, more even than Wilde and Hopkins, Joyce sees the end of literature as being the dynamic sharing of the heights and depths of the necessarily lonely unique Word—i.e., the self. Shem's word for this is "Astroglodynamono-logos" (*FW* 194), the stars and caves of the dynamic and lonely word.

Both Satan and Christ were self-exiled in upon their egos, but in contrasting ways. Christ is infinitely more mysterious than is Satan, to a Catholic if not to a Milton. Satan as a finite being is, like every self in Catholic vision, able to say "yes" or "no," which, as Hopkins well demonstrates in his mighty *Deutschland,* means that he chooses unity and infinite expanding with God or chooses lonely and limited autonomy. Satan, as Milton and Hopkins powerfully express, cannot reach that "worst" which would be his good, the point beyond which no worse could come to him. By his own choice he is condemned to plumb the bottomless chaos of nothingness forever. Joyce reflects this kind of exile in, among others, James Duffy and Stephen.

We have seen Duffy, like the Satan of the Gospels, demanding adoration in his usurpation of the confessional power bestowed upon the Apostles and their heirs, and realizing, while the hellish worm with fiery head winds through the darkness, that he is alone. Stephen assures Cranly—in their theological discussion (*P* 509–20) which climaxes the "man" part of *Portrait's* title, as the villanelle passage climaxes the "artist" part—that his "non serviam" is deliberate and not, in any Meredithian sense, sentimental, and that he is willing, if need be, to be alone forever. His actual nightlong shaking and noonday terror, the essential cowardliness which his role as Siegfried with Nothung will, in Joycean paradox, both satirize and negate, reveal to the perceptive reader, if not to Cranly, Stephen's refusal to see what is clear to Catholic vision—that Cranly spoke of Christ as the one ultimate friend, and that Stephen deliberately evades this obvious fact in projecting the possibility of homosexual interest into his really concerned and evidently heterosexual friend.

Such hellish solipsism, with the mind as its own place making its own heavens and hells, is the deadend street down which Stephen wanders until, as I now understand the matter, his paternalistic Ariadne, Bloom, sent his echoing feet down the limited but revealing Gaelic-Jew's harp alley to reach Tara via Holyhead. In some such devious way, not by a Pauline street called Straight, could Stephen ever arrive at the kind of heavenly "solipsism" enjoyed by Christ and, analogously, by Shem. Such "solus ipse" existence brings completion, not frustration, since it operates in a Trinitarian context. In the Trinity, as especially the Gospel of John reveals, the Son finds his completion in the Father, and in the perfection of their unity they breathe forth a Third Person, the Spirit properly named Love.[1]

Everybody sees this Trinitarian doctrine operative in the relationships of Bloom, Stephen, and Molly, but less obvious is the esthetic principle that as the fulfillment of divine being is found in God's contemplation and expression of himself, so the fulfillment of the literary artist's being is found in his contemplation and expression of himself. Joyce builds on this principle, realizing the difference between infinite and finite being, but realizing equally well that the human being images God in delighting in his own being, so long as he does not make that limited being his absolute end. Thus in a work of fine art, which really is nothing other than a human being in proper operation, the delight comes in my contemplation of myself in operation. When I enjoy Purcell's music, I have become that music, made as it is of materials proper to my ear, imagination, and intellect. I perceive myself in proper operation, and I am thrilled. I can go on to realize, as Hopkins does, that I have come as close as can be to becoming Purcell, to "sharing" the human experience which he managed to express in the counterpointed sound I have become. Purcell had to do it by contemplating himself, and by rejoicing in that. His work was not at all done primarily in relation to me, but could have been done wholly because he found delight in it himself. Hopkins's image of the great bird solely concentrating on the perfection of its flight and accidentally, in raising its wing, giving me insight into the kind of bird it is,[2] expresses something more than Purcell's concentration on the perfection of his art and his accidental stamping his own individual feature upon it. Purcell managed to reach to the basic experience of human nature, if one wishes to imagine it in some such Jungian way, or, in more Aristotelean terms that appealed to Joyce in expressing why he thought Dublin contained all cities, Purcell pierced through the individual to the universal—or, like Shem, he proceeded from individual order to dividual chaos (*FW* 186), where the creative Spirit could move upon the waters and bring forth a new cosmos, a new heaven and a new earth which can be shared by all who, with a grain of goodwill, will open themselves to the potentialities of their own being.

Some such operation of "the mystery of himsel"—where "himself" loses its "f" as "wasterpaperbaskel" changes its "t" (*FW* 194), so that "El" can be more clearly expressed—goes on inside Stephen as, alienated from Simon, he begins to see in himself at least some possibility of the good he experiences in Bloom. He is something like a fallen and selfish Christ, like the speaker of *CM,* No. 27, inexperienced in unselfish love, beginning to make contact with the loving Father who could alone bring him to know a completing union, and to feel a delight in human solipsism which might inform ink creatively. Then there emerges not a stillbirth, like the product of Mary Shortall and Jimmy Pidgeon in "Circe" (*U* 520)—which I see, as an analogue to the *Portrait's* villanelle, as a stillbirth proceeding from the idiotically Mariolatrous Stephen as father and the drooling Virgin, the Madonna-whore, of his diseased imagination as mother—but a vital and "immortal" creative work expressing as in *Ulysses* the experience of conscious and subconscious human experience and sinking and soaring even beyond the subnescious in *Finnegans Wake.* Such a winged work can rise from the moving waters, can pass like the divine Orion from human urine to quintessential fire.

In the Trinity, the Son, as it were, sinks into himself and finds two other persons. Shaun most clearly does this, as he sinks into the levels of himself, and among the many facts and unfacts that led Joyce to this particular insight, one is his broodings on the Mystery of the Trinity, the central mystery of the faith he could not swallow all of. Here, like the Shaunian Patrick of the final chapter of *FW,* Joyce found the three which complete the infinitely perfect one. Shem, in the rending of the rocks, knew himself as the man who is not a man (*FW* 170), one of the reasons being that he is more than one man. In an analogy with the Trinity, where any one Person is in complete loving communion with two Others, the artist finds himself in loving communion with the characters brought forth in the ink in which he operates. He can find completion in himself, unable in his creative act to accept anything from outside and not desirous to do so. He must, in fact, like Stephen fight against the voices which come to direct and determine his creativity. He is, as artist, satisfied with himself and with his expression of himself, like the Joyce Nora used to hear laughing in the next room during the night as he produced the perfect distortions in his chambermade music expressing the solipsistic Joyce, analogue of the solipsistic divine Word in the Trinity, revolving in our human literary cosmos. We can, if with goodwill we choose to do so, bring forth, during our ideal insomnia, all that chambermade upheaval within ourselves, and thus enjoy ourselves in operation, like Hamlet reading the book of himself, and shudder with Hamlet and wonder with Bottom over what dreams may come or seem to have come. Then we will experience what literature is, not in the certitude of facts, but in the boundless and fascinating mystery inclusive of unfacts.

On the two following pages, *FW* 185–86, Joyce builds the profoundest and most beautiful image of the literary artist that (if I may indulge myself in a risk of overstatement) our literature has known. He pictures the artist, the descendant of the "old artificer" of *Portrait* (here the "opifex, altus prosator") making his caustic ink in a Grecian Urn from the waste materials of his own body, and writing on his own skin the dynamic experience of his exiled self. Everything he writes is in the present tense, "one continuous present tense integument," the expression of a being in progress, and since it is his whole history it expresses also the whole of human history, the universal being included in the particular. He is exiled upon his own ego, as God is, and thus like God, he experiences himself as "El," the center of his own interior universe, the "Ego," or "I am" which is the proper name of God, the basis of all being.[3] The furniture in which Shem writes himself is most properly his ink, furnished by his body and biting into his body, like the ancient, mysterious writing sunk into the ass's skin in Balzac's *Peau de chagrin,* the novel involved in the adjective "chagreenold" of *FW* 186. He is in that ink more intimately than was Dorian in the paint of the picture in which his soul was somehow infused. Joyce pictures the artist gradually shrinking and fading in his physical being, "waned chagreenold and doriangrayer," until his body disappears altogether into nothingness, "dudhud," and his soul remains, like Dorian's operative in the paint, operative in the ink he had, like a squid, shot out from himself to screen himself from the universe outside himself.[4] That ink (and, presumably, the skin, the foolscap in which it was etched) remains with its colors, beauty, and cosmic meaning (as does the ink of the *Book of Kells* etched into skin), and in that ink, like Christ in the Eucharist, the artist continues in a dynamic present to unfold the cycles of his and all human history.

The eucharistic image, built up throughout Joyce's work, comes to its climactic point in the participle, "transaccidentated." From that Romantic chalice of "Araby" to the brimming chalice of the villanelle is not a long journey, though a good deal of realism has been picked up (or perhaps, made actual) on the way. The Dracula tonalities of the villanelle's chalice were foreshadowed, after all, in *CM*, No. 27, and stressed in the poisonous and stinging insect images applied to women (climaxing in Floh and Luse and Bienie and Vespatilla of *FW* 414), and woven throughout in the bats associated with Irish women, with May in Stephen's memories as he cribs Hyde's elegant Englishing of Connaught emotions (*U* 48), with Gertie and Molly in Bloom's swooning consciousness at the end of "Nausicaa," and again climactically with the description (as I take it to be) of *FW* as "Dracula's nightout" (*FW* 145). The blood of Stephen brimming in that ambivalent chalice of the villanelle's mass, a foreshadowing of the white and black masses so structurally important in *Ulysses,* lays a basis for Shem's blood and body becoming, through transaccidentation rather than transsubstantiation, the consecrated ink of the artist, finally achieving that "priest of eternal imagination" status that Stephen had aspired to.

The white masses (meaning actual or imagined masses honoring God, the positive aspect of Catholic devotion) are few in *Ulysses,* though the Catholic attitude toward the mass is vitally operative throughout, and gives the necessary basis for perception of the activity of the black masses. Buck's opening consecration, while it lampoons Catholic attitudes and confects a transvestite Christ, should be considered in the white category, I judge, since it is a parody of the mass which celebrates the union with the Father. Buck as scientist pokes fun at the Catholic theory which tried to account for the Real Presence in terms of medieval notions of substance and accident, as he pretends that the Power (the Holy Spirit, the Third Person of the Trinity, who is the Power which overshadowed Mary and the Power which effects the sacraments) has managed to dislodge the substance of the wine (or in this case of the shaving lather) and squeeze in all of Christ's substance and of all his accidents except the white corpuscles. Those are important to Buck, I suppose, because they enter so largely into the diseases he was studying, and to Joyce because they play a part in the Pale Vampire image weaving through his imagination.[5] In any case, Buck initiates his patronizing and destructive campaign against Stephen the true artist by indicating, like Shaun claiming to be a better artist than Shem, that he can be both a better and a funnier priest of the imagination that Stephen ever can.

Taken for granted behind that funny and profound first page of *Ulysses* is Catholic doctrine on the operation of the three persons in the Trinity, on the Incarnation of the Second Person, and on the nature and operation of the Eucharist. Joyce is out to express Irish experience, which, as he told James Stephens, is Catholic, and therefore not expressible by a Protestant.[6] Something of the same thing is true about what I see as the profoundest depths of Joyce's esthetic as it assumes flesh in his creative words. Unless it is seen against the positive as well as the negative aspects of Catholic feeling and thought and aspiration, it may appear as distorted or as shallow. Joyce as artist takes no polemical position. He is out to express his experience, a complex of many things, among them an experience and a knowledge of the positive aspects of Catholicism. He did not see Catholicism as simply an evil force frustrating and repressing the self. He did of course see that aspect, but he saw it against the background of Catholic aspiration to fulfill and complete the self beyond the limits of nature, even infinitely beyond. That background is the necessary foil for seeing the depth of the patterning of Buck's burlesque of the artist transmuting the daily bread of his human experience into the radiant body of everliving life. "Transmuting" is Stephen's insertion of alchemy into his otherwise Catholic image (*P* 490). Catholic tradition had ruled out that term dripping with alchemical superstition in favor of "transsubstantiation," a useful coinage to express a Catholic effort to deal on nonalchemical terms with a transcendent mystery, and itself, according to a number of theologians both Catholic and Protestant, unfortunately saturated with some pseudoscientific medieval superstition.[7] But the Catholic grasp of Christ's love and power in instituting a symbol that was also a living and dynamic reality, a food and a union of lovers all in one, is the deepest and most valuable element in Joyce's expression of the nature of literature and of the function of the Real Presence of the literary artist in his ink.

Bloom watches a real Catholic mass in All Hallows, and in Bloom's acute but uninformed perception it naturally looks shallow, blind, and hypocritical. The priest, associate of those deft-fingered and smiling sinister figures which loom throughout *Portrait,* smartly drinks off the dregs of Christ's blood before he efficiently and swiftly cleans things up. Bloom had connected the "corpus" (which he heard as the priest recited the Communion formula, stressing in brisk hurry the first word, "Corpus Domini Nostri Jesu Christi custodiat animam tuam in vitam aeternam, Amen," as he gave out the host which alone was available then to the laity) with advertising, and thought that such stress on the body was part of the priest's assumed cleverness in deceiving these women pretending modest piety. The male body would be attractive both to these women (and to Molly, who yearned for a Narcissus and for swimming boys like naked gods) and to cannibals. Father Conmee would soon utilize both appeals in this very church, speaking on the African missions, and Bloom anticipates the final chapter of *FW* in seeing the connection with St. Patrick's clever use of the shamrock as he came to the Irish mission. Joyce too will make later use in Mulligan's black mass of Bloom's observation of the kneeling priest's "large grey bootsole from under the lace affair he had on" (*U* 81). The Reverend Mr. Haines Love, taking the place of the serving breezes of the first page, raises the celebrant's "petticoat" and reveals "his grey bare hairy buttocks between which a carrot is stuck" as he translates "Corpus Meum" into "my body" (*U* 599). Thus the Catholic threads weave through the great patterning of Joyce's work.

Stephen's mass in "Oxen" is also, on the whole, a white one. Like Christ at the head of the first Catholic altar on the first Holy Thursday, "young Stephen that had mien of a frere . . . was at head of the board" (*U* 388). He "filled all cups that stood empty" except, apparently, Bloom's, and spoke words which, when I wrote of this matter some years ago, I had to confess were puzzling and obscure to me: "Now drink we, quod he, of this mazer and quaff ye this mead which is not indeed parcel of my body but my soul's bodiment" (*U* 391). My best guess then was that Stephen meant "also that the drink gives body to his soul by giving him energy and courage to bring forth the word."[8] As a result of brooding over the development of the eucharistic image, particularly of Joyce's use of it in *FW,* I believe I now understand what is in Stephen's mind. His use of "mazer," first of all, derives from his image of himself as a Hamlet figure, since Hamlet used the word, in a slightly different form, to denote a skull cast up by the gravedigger: "And now my Lady Worm's, chapless, and knocked about the mazzard with a sexton's spade. Here's fine revolution" (5. 1. 96–98). The word fits the period the "Oxen" passage imitates and foreshadows the "carl on the kopje" who "is slaking nuncheon out of some thing's brain pan" (*FW* 15). This reference to the history of the word, perhaps founded in some historical instances of using enemies' skulls as drinking vessels somewhat as His Majesty the Alaki does with the skull of his predecessor in "Cyclops" (*U* 334), bridges the use of the mazer as holder of the metaphorical Eucharist in "Oxen" and the use of the contents of the artist's head as source for the "radiant body of everliving life" of literature: "and, an you could peep inside the cerebralised saucepan of this eer illwinded goodfornobody, you would see in his house of thoughtsam (was you, that is, decontaminated enough to look discarnate) what a jetsam litterage of convolvuli of times lost or strayed" (*FW* 292). The thing we must be decontaminated from is the body, which, in Joyce's image of the artist's transaccidentation, must go, so that the soul will be free to inform the ink. Thus we too, if we are to see into the artist's brainpan, must achieve the opposite of the Incarnation which made possible Christ's Eucharist, and at least look in discarnate fashion at the magic ink.

Now, I believe, I am in a position to explain why Stephen's mead is not parcel of his body, since he, unlike Christ in the Eucharist, has none of his "mortal coil" along with him. In Catholic teaching, the whole Christ, substance and accidents, is present under the form of bread and of wine. In Joyce's image, only the soul, the substantial form, of the artist is present, his accidents having passed ("trans-") into nothingness. And thus Stephen's mead is his soul's bodiment, because again unlike Christ, who undergoes no change at all, the artist acquires a new "body" in which his soul will operate, namely his ink, which is now informed with the disembodied substance of the artist. His new body is the letters of the alphabet, "a jetsam litterage," which provide for his individual person a new principle of individuation, a dividual chaos of "litters from aloft," from which the creative spirit can shape lives not livable by the individual artist in his own body: "(thereby, he said, reflecting from his own individual person life unlivable, transaccidentated through the slow fires of consciousness into a dividual chaos, perilous, potent, common to allflesh, human only, mortal)" (*FW* 186). In the sentence following, "Leave ye fraction of bread to them that live by bread alone" (*U* 391), Stephen picks up the imagery operative from "The Sisters" on, based on the fact that only the priest, in Catholic practice of his time, received the consecrated wine. Here Stephen claims for himself and his disciples gathered around the board that priesthood which, as the spiritual director frenetically orated to the potential future Jesuit in *Portrait,* makes the priest more powerful than the Blessed Virgin herself. Stephen will go on, on this and the following page, to claim such superiority to Mary. He also, in this sentence, urges his followers to leave the ritual breaking of bread to the "lewd," the laity, who cannot get at the wine and thus, in Stephen's bitter and clever wit, become not like the divine Christ but like the hungry and thirsty Christ in the desert, rejecting

Satan's suggestion that he turn the rocks into bread with the statement, which Stephen paraphrases, that the word of God is more nourishing than bread alone. Stephen hints also at the notion that he intends to develop, that the word of God, the divine creator, is really deficient in comparison with the human word of the true artist. More valuable than the mere natural creation attributed to God is the "postcreation" clearly proceeding from the artist, wherein "omnis caro" comes to the artist and is given inky immortality. I suppose that Stephen echoes his previous use of the phrase from Psalm 65 (and the funeral mass) on page 48, where it was in a Dracula context, partly because operative in his mind here is his notion of a priestly exchange of blood for ink.

Another notion most important here, developed later in several ways, is the notion of artist as caller-forth of ghosts, who will come trooping from Hades at his call, to receive new inky life that will not pass away. For Stephen this notion reaches its climax, as I can now see the matter, when at the sound of the bells of St. George both he and Bloom, whose waters had just met in creative flow, find their previous depression in thoughts of death pointed now toward new life as well as a new dawn—pointed, at least, toward the possibility of new life. Stephen, on *U* 704, now hears the prayers for the dying in a four-part skipping rhythm which will sound out from his retreating feet, on their way, as I have tried to establish, to Tara. His sterile "Oxen" mass has been superseded, or perhaps completed, by the mass celebrated by Bloom, in which the cream of Molly enriched the cocoa god-food and brought this Trinity of Father and Son and Love into at least the potential of conferring life both upon inky ghosts (proceeding from the Son) and upon human flesh (possibly proceeding from the Father and Love).

Buck's black mass, produced, apparently, in Stephen's imagination, has as one of its sources the connection Stephen established earlier between roguewords and monkwords. Stephen at this point in "Circe," having fled after striking at Bella's light, now ecstatically celebrates not the Temptress of the Villanelle but simple Cissy Caffrey. Some of the ecstasy, I suspect, flows from his perception of how perfectly Cissy can be expressed in the words proper to the Canting Academy of the thievish gypsies, roguewords every bit as good as monkwords, Stephen had thought in "Proteus" (*U* 47). The thought of monkwords and the celebration of Love, mixed with military elements, carry Stephen's thoughts back to Malachi Mulligan's opening mass on the first page. The prophet Malachi, scriptural forerunner of Buck, brought to a close the Old Testament, and in so doing expressed, in a passage Catholics take to be prophetic of the universal daily celebration of the mass—"For from the rising of the sun to its setting my name is great among the nations, and in every place incense is offered to my name, and a pure offering" (Mal. 1:11)—the image which Stephen and Joyce adopt as expressive of the artist's proper activity, the offering of pure musical words in praise of eternal Imagination. Buck, as he did in the opening lines of the book, affects the monkwords, this time addressed to the devil, and Haines Love, as opposed in his Anglican soul to the Latin as was Mr. Fogarty in his Greek-Orthodox Photian soul in "Grace,"[9] translates at once into English. This kind of religious attitude expressed in choice of language explains the choice of somewhat degraded Latin in the climactic image of the artist as priest on *FW* 185, where the preparation of the ink to be consecrated is in monkwords so that the Anglican ordinal may not feel the cheeky blush which Haines in chapter 1 ought to feel but of which he is so snobbishly unaware.

Buck's elevation of the blood-dripping host carries us back to Bloom's musings on *U* 80. The custom was for the priest to make the sign of the cross with the host as he lifted it from the ciborium before placing it on the tongue of the communicant. Bloom the phenomenologist, observing this and deducing (erroneously, as phenomenologists like psychoanalysts are prone to do) that the "communion" was in liquid ("are they in water?"), foreshadows Buck the scientific pseudo-artist, removing the "corpus" from the blood. Bloom, as he in imagination lies in his bath water, sees himself, as Stephen in "Eumaeus" and "Ithaca" apparently begins to see him, as a true Messiah in water—"This is my body" (*U* 86). Bloom celebrates a white mass with Stephen in the kitchen, and goes upstairs, having lighted Malachian incense for his own more intimate sacrifice, to celebrate (or, perhaps, to complete) his own climactic mass, combining the elements of the white and the black masses of the book, on "that living altar where the back changes name" (*U* 551).

Bloom's interest in rear ends is stressed in the opening lines of his existence, as with kindly interest he observes the lithe black form of the cat, Molly's "familiar," in "Ithaca" to be so closely identified with Milly (*U* 693). The cream which he liturgically prepares for Stephen and the warm-bubbled milk he pours for the pussens and sets slowly on the floor seem to me related aspects of Bloom's white-black mass, as does his interest in "the white button under the butt of her tail" (*U* 55) in relation to the black button which ends Bloom's existence at the conclusion of "Ithaca." The *osculum infame* was a standard principal part of the medieval black mass, as Jeffrey Burton Russell makes abundantly clear in his splendid study, *Witchcraft in the Middle Ages*:[10] "If the Christians had their creed, their Eucharist, their kiss of peace, the witches formally forswore the faith, confected obscene parodies of the sacrament, and bestowed kisses upon the Devil's fundament" (278-79). "The Devil appears in the form of a toad, goose, or duck, as a black cat with erect tail which descends a statue backwards to meet his worshipers, or as a thin, pale man with black, shining eyes. The postulant kisses the apparition either on the mouth or on the anus. When he has done, the master of the sect, and then the other initiates, also give the obscene kiss" (160-61). Joyce knew the background of the black mass from many sources, perhaps from some of its Dublin practitioners and some of the Triestine adepts. Huysman's work was of interest to Joyce as it had been to Dorian Gray, and the kind of fascinated interest such cult films as *Rosemary's Baby* and *The Exorcist* rouse in current moviegoers found at least equal welcome in Joyce's environment. The kiss of peace took on more importance in the diabolical liturgy than in the Catholic mass, for reasons Russell sets forth: "The kiss is a symbol of eating the beloved, and the kiss had enormous importance in Christian art, literature, and liturgy, even symbolizing the Holy Spirit's binding of the Father and the Son. . . . The kiss is the link between the sexual in witchcraft and the cannibalistic devouring of children" (285–86). Thus Bloom's nightly homage has interest for liturgists as well as for psychoanalysts. Most important of all, perhaps, is the suggestion that Molly as Holy Spirit effects the binding of Bleephan. And the masses of *Ulysses*, developing all aspects of the complex mass elements suggested in Stephen's villanelle, are brought to a satisfying unity in the final mass offered by Bloom, white in its sincere adoration of the anus of the goddess, black in its tendency toward a bestial exclusion of the divine.

Huysmans indicates two categories of black mass: " 'But,' said Durtal, 'in the Middle Ages the mass was celebrated in a different fashion. The altar then was the naked buttocks of a woman; in the seventeenth century it was the abdomen.' "[11] Buck, who had indicated his procedure in Hellenizing the island by bringing forth, like Zeus, his bestially seventeenth-century *Everyman His own Wife,* gives us a seventeenth-century black mass on Mina's fruitful abdomen. Leopold reaches further back into Christian and anti-Christian tradition for his own homage; having honored the human word in his communion with Stephen, he honors human flesh in his partial communion with Molly. I suppose it is possible to judge that he also degrades both the word and the flesh, but if the whole context of his activity is included, it seems to me that Poldy rather elevates the human than pulls down the divine. Buck, on the other hand, appears to me, in his clever manipulation both of word and (especially if Stephen's hints at Buck's homosexual designs are justified) of flesh, really destructive of the human, and as a result degrading as well to the divine.[12]

For Joyce, all these masses give honor to the goddess he worshipped, the divine Imagination. In the frustrated Stephen, Joyce the artist expressed in Stephen's wet dream his physical desires and in his bloated villanelle his imperfect worship. In the even more frustrated Shem, Joyce expresses once again in the marks of emission and in the ink of *Finnegans Wake* his far more perfect worship: "The specks on his lapspan are his foul deed thougths, wishmarks of mad imogenation" (*FW* 251). Stephen in "Scylla and Charybdis" had established his own temporal identity by means of the mole on his right breast (*U* 194), which he carries with him through all the physical flux of time, as he pictures Shakespeare carrying with him the cinque-spotted mole of Imogen, really the expression of his own "vorrei e non vorrei" experience with Ann, the human experience which made possible the creation of Lucrece and Imogen (*U* 197). Now Shakespeare is a ghost, a shadow, like the elder Hamlet, and exists only in his ink—or rather, the Shakespeare of this book exists in Stephen, who exists in the ink which operates by the informing existence of James Joyce. Which means, in the end, that Shakespeare exists in James Joyce, as Stephen does (which we see symbolized in Bella Cohen's Wildean mirror), and we may come to realize, if mad imogenation blesses us, that James Joyce can exist in us.

The image of the Eucharist is one of the ways Joyce seeks to express his Wildean notions of the presence of the artist in his work, and above all to preach his own gospel of the possibility of communion between an artist and a reader. Catholic doctrine preaches that through the faithful and loving reception of the consecrated host, a Christian can literally become Christ, can share in the divine act of being. Joyce wants to preach, analogously, that through the goodwilled reproduction of the artist's words in one's imagination, one can share in the human experience of the artist, and the artist himself can be said to be living by means of the reader's (or better, the hearer's) own act of existence.

Some of the thoughts weaving through the mind of Joyce as he brought Stephen's mass of "Oxen of the Sun" into being show up in the Herring notes for "Oxen" (*Herring* 185). The third note deals with the Blessed Virgin and her conception and pregnancy, and with the dilemma Stephen presents about the bad results of her knowing or not knowing her lover, who became her son (the drunken Stephen will in a Mulligan tonality attempt to introduce a notion of indecency here). The note in *Herring* reads: "(?WM: motherhood ?immune from joy and pain. If she knew her love awkward. If not her ?ignorance & her manifestation of love is indecent)." The passage in *Ulysses* reads: "Or she knew him, that second I say, and was but creature of her creature, *vergine madre figlia di tuo figlio* or she knew him not and then stands she in the one denial or ignorancy with Peter Piscator who lives in the house that Jack built and with Joseph the Joiner patron of the happy demise of all unhappy marriages *parce que M. Léo Taxil nous a dit que qui l'avait mise dans cette fichue position c'était le sacré pigeon, ventre de Dieu*! *Entweder* transsubstantiality *oder* consubstantiality but in no case subsubstantiality" (*U* 391). Stephen is asserting the artist's superiority over Mary as producer of the Word, and he wants to suggest that her relationship with God, with some of the metaphysical complexities indicated in the Dantean conception of "daughter of your son," was that of a woman being treated as a whore by her son (Stephen's ultimate degradation of his own madonna-whore construct), or it was that of a woman deceived by her divine lover, who comes upon her as a damned pigeon rather than as a Jovian swan. Then follow with German solemnity the eucharistic terms stressing the connection in Stephen's mind between the Annunciation, in which the Word became flesh, and the Eucharist, in which Christ offers himself, substance and accidents, to his lovers.

The following note in *Herring* suggests what might have been transpiring in Joyce's creating imagination: "transsubstantiality combated by Duns Scotus" (p. 185). I believe that what happened was something like this: Joyce lists three terms in the "Oxen" passage. "Transsubstantiality" is the Catholic term, designed especially to indicate the substantial presence of the whole Christ under the appearances of bread and of wine. "Consubstantiality" is the Lutheran term, or maybe better Wycliffian term, indicating that both substances are present, so that Christ and bread and Christ and wine are totally present. "Subsubstantiality" I take to be a vulgar coinage of Stephen's, inspired by Mulligan's crude ballad and by Taxil's cruder notions, and by the charge of Celsus referred to in "Circe" (*U* 521) concerning an affair between Mary and a Roman soldier named Panther. He is probably thinking of some "beast with two backs" notion, and adapts the eucharistic term to the bestiality to which Mulligan reduces all "beastly dead" humanity.

Joyce's note reveals that he thought that Scotus combated the Thomistic explanation of the Real Presence. I cannot discover where Joyce most likely ran into this matter, nor where he learned about the term "transaccidenta-tion," which as a matter of fact Scotus seems to have been the first to use. He used it, indeed, in the context of the Thomistic "transsubstantiation," but not, in so far as I can determine, in any combating of the Thomistic position. The *OED* traces the history of the word, but apparently, in the judgment of my friend David Hayman, who surely knows more than anyone else about the dating of the first drafts of *FW,* Joyce wrote the "transaccidentation" passage before he could have seen the *OED*'s rather sketchy history of the word. There are plenty of other possible sources, certainly, but I have been so far unable to tie them up with Joyce. I suspect that Joyce, in reading about or discussing with some learned seminarian in a Paris bar the history of the Eucharist, heard that Wycliffe had picked up the Scotian term in order to batter the "new" and, to a right-wing reactionary like Wycliffe, "heretical" mixing of Greek concepts of science with the established and properly unscientific teaching of the pre-Aristoteleans.

Scotus, who did oppose Thomas in many important ways, did not at all object to Thomas's term "transsubstantiation," and merely introduces the term "transaccidentation," in the passage cited by the *OED,* in order to indicate that a discussion of the transition of accidents need not enter into the doctrine. The Thomistic explanation stresses the disappearance of the substance of the bread (a concept quite possible in the scientific approach of his time, not so readily accessible in ours) and the continued presence of two sets of accidents, Christ's (present but not operating as they did during his life on earth, as ours do now—present, in the Thomistic impressive term "per modum substantiae," in the mode of that which "stands under," or is hidden) and the bread's, which continue in some mysterious fashion to operate as if they had not lost their substance. This fancy "miracle" drove Wycliffe into a gradual crescendo of frenzy, and he insisted that if there were such a thing as transsubstantiation, there would also be transaccidentation, since the appearance of a thing without the existence of the thing seemed to him, in his pre-Alice in Wonderland simplicity, contradictory.

I am, by the way, trying to approach this matter as I suppose the imagination of Joyce to have done, not at all as I conceive a theologian to do. Theologians do not operate on the basis of imagination, when they operate properly, and would not be inclined, for example, to see "per modum substantiae" as I depict it above. I am convinced that it was the quality of invisibility that was most of all operative for Joyce, however, because he was thinking of the artist as like the god of creation, invisible; like Christ in the Eucharist, invisible in and under his artistic ink; like the stone heliotrope, answer to the riddle that Shem must but cannot solve, which magically makes the owner invisible (cf. *OED* under "heliotrope"), and distantly ties in with May Dedalus's enjoyment of Turko the Terrible as the boy who enjoyed invisibility (*U* 10). The concerns of theologians like Ockham (*U* 40) with the other problems that enter into the discussion of transsubstantiation, such things as multilocation, the operation of matter, the effects of time and space, the acts of existence of substance and of accidents, and the like, were of interest to Joyce in so far as he could wrest them into the capacious limits of his imagination. He was not much concerned if he ignored or damaged theological principle. If he could find some basis for advancing the cause of divine Imagination, he would accept and manipulate any theological term which served him. He is not, like a theologian, interested in dealing with the truth outside his own being. He is exclusively interested, like an artist, in expressing the true which he finds flowing through his own being.

Joyce may well have run into the Lutheran development of the Wycliffian use of "transaccidentation" also. In using the term, Scotus was merely concerned with explaining Thomas's position, with which, at least in the passage cited in the *OED* and the few others I have managed to track down, he does not disagree. Luther like Wycliffe wants to quarrel with Thomas's position that the two natures or substances cannot coexist in the sacrament, since, as one of the arguments puts it, the singular subject of "This is my body" cannot refer to both Christ's body and the substance of the bread. Luther attacks that argument by pointing out that if we must say that transsubstantiaiton takes place lest the "this" refer to both substances, we had better also have transaccidentation, lest the "this" refer to both accidents. A Catholic response, and one that would assist Joyce's own eucharistic image, might be that it is obvious to the senses that the "this" refers to the accidents of the bread which I hold, and that thus transaccidentation, which has been desired or imagined by the superstitious from time to time as a sensible proof of the transsubstantiation (thus the stories of the bleeding hosts, the priest holding a tiny baby, and the like), is seen by the eyeballs to be nonexistent.

The logical dilemma Luther presents is therefore a fallacy, ignoring Christ's intent (a poetic as well as a sacramental one, to provide an attractive symbol of complete corporal union as well as effecting it in reality) and the nature of the sacrament. Transaccidentation would destroy the sacrament, doing away with the symbol and nullifying the reason for Christ's establishing the sacrament—i.e., to serve as food for his lovers.[13]

Wherever Joyce may have found "transaccidentation," the notion it expresses fits perfectly into the context of the mass of "Oxen," and as it is used on *FW* 186, explicates the puzzling statement, "quaff ye this mead which is not indeed parcel of my body but my soul's bodiment" (*U* 391). Stephen is thinking of the mead as the symbol of the artist's ink and comparing the activity of the artist in his ink with that of Christ under the appearance of wine (or of bread). In Catholic teaching, the whole Christ, body and soul, is present under both species. There is no substance of the bread or of the wine, but only the miraculously supported accidents (this is the explanation Joyce learned; it is not held by all Catholic theologians). Hence, in the consecrated chalice, we have one substance (Christ's) and two sets of accidents (Christ's operating *per modum substantiae* and the wine's, continuing to operate as they did before the change). Stephen therefore is not saying that this wine (or mead) is not my body because my body is in or under the appearance of bread. He is saying that my body is not in or under this mead because my body has done what, in the Eucharist, the substance of the wine has done, i.e., disappeared. We see that happening to Shem on *FW* 186: "with each word that would not pass away the squidself which he had squirtscreened from the crystalline world waned chagreenold and doriangrayer in its dudhud." The squid squirts out its ink from itself as Shem does, both as the ink which forms the world and as his own blood, as in the Eucharist. He thus loses his color (the flag of Ireland, for one thing, green and "or" and gray, his white not quite arrived until all his blood-ink is gone) and advances into physical nonbeing, the dudhud of Finnegan—cf. *FW* 499: "but your saouls to the dhaoul, do ye. Finnk. Fime. Fudd?"

Joyce was also thinking of his fading eyesight, which may be suggested, along with the Miltonic cosmos, in that "crystalline world." He wrote to Miss Weaver in September, 1928, of his warding off blindness "by dressing in the three colours of cecity as the Germans divide them" (*Letters,* 2:269), that is, green, gray, and black. The gradual fading as the result of his willing destruction of his body in the service of art fits perfectly with the shrinking ass's skin in Balzac's *Peau de chagrin,* the tale of a magic skin, into which Sanskrit letters were deeply etched, giving power to the owner but shrinking with each choice the owner made. When it disappeared, the owner would die. Balzac's novel was a forerunner of *The Picture of Dorian Gray,* and the moral switch between the picture of Dorian and the evil and selfish person himself obviously fits Shem's identification of himself with his ink. So Stephen's words in "Oxen" become clear when we see that, unlike the passing of substance in the real Eucharist, the artist suffers a passing of accident so that his substance may enter into the ink and operate there as in a new body. Thus in the artistic consecrated ink of the artist, there are two substances but only one set of accidents. The artist's accidents have faded altogether away, and his substance has entered *in,* not under, the ink. Here we have consubstantiation,[14] but not conaccidentation. This new magic being is the ink just as it was, substance and accidents, but now marvelously informed by the artist's substance, his form, his soul, so that, like Christ in the Eucharist, he can share his now everliving life with all who love him enough to form his words and music in themselves.

To express the presence of the artist under his ink or under his page, Joyce uses many devices. One of the most interesting is found in Justius's charge to Mercius to stop hiding behind the covering of words and to show himself in his true colors: "Stand forth, Nayman of Noland (for no longer will I follow you obliquelike through the inspired form of the third person singular and the moods and hesitensies of the deponent" (*FW* 187). Justius accuses Mercius of being negative and unpatriotic, but I seem to sense two other images lurking in the terms being used. The Nayman strikes me as echoing the Mr. Nemo (Nobody) of the "Cyclops" incident, when Odysseus hid beneath the sheep so that the blinded Cyclops could not find him by feeling on the surface, like us if we merely run our eyes over the stained sheepskin (or calfskin) of the *Book of Kells.* His acting like a deponent, passive in form but active in meaning, strikes me as describing the artist in his ink, passive on the surface (so that the blond cop of the previous page who could find nothing but ink was bright in the main) but dynamically active underneath, as Christ is under the appearances of bread and wine. Thus the artist, the Homo Made Ink of *FW* 342, operates powerfully in the ideal world of literature, and leaves the rationalist, whose "downright there you are and there it is is only all in his eye" (*FW* 118), to grope his one-leveled way in the unreal shadows of "reality."

I find in Joyce's esthetic as it expresses itself in the eucharistic image an answer to the question, "Who is the dreamer in *Finnegans Wake?*" I agree that it is L. Boom, as Benstock has suggested, and that it is Shakespeare, as Mrs. Glasheen perceptively argues, and I think it is Finn McCool, the giant lying under Dublin beside the Liffey, but beyond all those and others, I judge it is basically Joyce himself, expressing himself as he told Stanislaus he was doing in *Dubliners,* as he often phrased his efforts in *Work in Progress,* as most of all he expresses Shem doing on *FW* 185–86. He dedicated his first play "To My Own Soul," he shows Stephen lost in his own inner self, bringing forth and contemplating his own literary cosmos with total satisfaction, an image of the Trinitarian Father blissful in His powerful generating of the Word and their mutual breathing forth infinite Love. The artist sharing his own experience in the music of his language reflects God's sharing of His infinitely beautiful experience with finite beings. Joyce well knows his experience is finite and his expression limited, but he knows too that it is music and can be counterpointed, like the mass for Pope Marcellus. Thus an inner cosmos, also in dynamic flux and many-leveled, can by some magic be expressed if both the ear and the eye operate and commingle, time and space, and kinetically feel, like frustrated Bottom, the mysterious motions of that which in Hopkins's "Spring and Fall": "Nor mouth had, no, nor mind expressed / What heart heard of, ghost guessed."

The poet who has faith in his human experience can break out of the determinism of the rationalists. The ancient poet, the "poeta," originally raided by barbarians as were the monks at Kells, expressed as Homer and Dante and Shakespeare did the basic and original reading, that mysterious primal sundering that left us alone but with a grieving longing for communion which has in itself a mysterious beauty. What reason cannot code can nevertheless be decorded—untied, drawn from the heart, broken into the unexpected chords and discords of counterpoint, reaching toward that mysterious blissful communion which St. Paul spoke of and Bottom paraphrased ("The eye of man hath not heard, the ear of man hath not seen"),[15] beyond anything we have lost and grieved for. Joyce always thought of his work as music,"this chambermade music" (FW 184), and the first words he published, "Strings in the earth and air/Make music sweet," sounded the music of Irish harp. Chamber Music, No. 3, speaks of the lover

alone
Awake to hear the sweet harps play
To Love before him on his way
And the night wind answering in antiphon
Till night is overgone?

That antiphon sings the death of night, but when the counterpoint sounds in Finnegans Wake, Joyce's holy Book of Kells, it reaches beyond death, and points toward ultimate mystery:

> He is cured by faith who is sick of fate. The prouts who will invent a writing there ultimately is the poeta, still more learned, who discovered the raiding there originally. That's the point of eschatology our book of kills reaches for now in soandso many counterpoint words. What can't be coded can be decorded if an ear aye sieze what no eye ere grieved for. (FW 482)

5 Joyce and the Jesuits

"Chuck Loyola, Kinch, and come on down" (*U* 9). Thus Buck advises "the jejune jesuit" (*U* 4) to descend from his sterile Ignatian knightly tower and to shake off his bitter Hamlet-brooding on the offenses to his wounded self. Shem too, in rhyming doggerel, is "dejected into day and night with jesuit bark and bitter bite" (*FW* 182). "Bark," like "belt" early in *Portrait,* yields two meanings, the medicinal Jesuit Bark from the trees in the Peru mission, which heals, and the bark of the Jesuit dog, whose bite poisons. That dog may be allied to the "Domini Canis" who reviewed *Ulysses* in the *Dublin Review* in 1922,[1] or perhaps more closely to the additional remarks of the Jesuit C. C. Martindale,[2] who found Joyce operating on "that level where seething instinct is not yet illuminated by intellect." Joyce does indeed operate on that level, but Father Martindale evidently senses an attack on the certainty and determined optimism of his own notion of Irish Catholicism. Shem, at any rate, feels the poisonous bite, far worse than the bark.

Throughout *Portrait,* the rich background for the production of the "orchidised" (*U* 425) Stephen emerges in the detailed portraits of the Jesuits. As the small Stephen made his fearful way through the "dark narrow corridor" leading to the rector's office (*P* 301), he felt the eyes of four centuries of historical Jesuits silently looking down on him from the pictures on the walls—Loyola with his A.M.D.G.; Francis Xavier pointing to his chest, symbolizing the divine fire of the Sacred Heart which he felt there; "Lorenzo Ricci with his berreta on his head"; the ever-youthful Kostka, Gonzaga, and Berchmans; and, bringing history to the present time and place, the founder of Clongowes, the revered Kenny.

Lorenzo Ricci presents his birettaed head in the articles about him both in the old *Catholic Encyclopedia* and the *New Catholic Encyclopedia*. He gets special attention in Stephen's mind, I suspect, not only because he was general of the society when it was suppressed, but because he could serve as something of a model for the more and more beleaguered Stephen. Soon after Ricci had been elected general in May of 1758, Clement XIII counseled him to take for his defense "Silentium, patientiam et preces." Silence, patience, and prayer. The earnest leader of the Jesuits repeated this watchword incessantly to his followers until he was imprisoned and silenced, and Stephen, like Joyce before him, was no doubt as familiar with his story as the rector of Belvedere supposed him to be with that of St. Francis Xavier (*P* 359). Thus when Stephen, threatened with suppression by many voices, with capture by many nets, took for his defense "silence, exile, and cunning" (*P* 519), he may very well have been imitating that threatened Jesuit whose eyes he felt in the dark corridor.

When an echo of Stephen's watchword, in religious context, shows up in *FW*, the "cunning" is specifically tied up with Ignatius Loyola, and the silence seems to involve patience in the person of the spider-watching Bruce: "the bruce, the coriolano and the ignacio" (*FW* 228). And having fought against all the seven sacraments (*FW* 227:29–36), Shem too is speaking as a general—Joyce would have no difficulty in spotting Jesuit characteristics in Dicken's confidence man, Alfred Jingle ("For he is the general, make no mistake in he. He is General Jinglesome" [*FW* 229]). The Ignatian general slides later into the Russian general mixed with the Jesuit general ("the figure of a fellowchap in the wohly ghast, Popey O'Donoshough, the jesuneral of the russuates" [*FW* 349]). Ricci, I suspect, appears in *Portrait* as something of a basis for all threatened generals, leaders of warriors, priests, or artists.

Joyce's novel, *Portrait,* focuses on a threatened artist. Hence sympathetic studies of Jesuits would threaten the tone and complicate the plot. In any event, none of the major depictions of Jesuits is sympathetic. A glance at the main figures, as we see them developing in the dark room of Stephen's consciousness, may help to clarify both the attitudes of Stephen and of his creator. Father Arnall, somewhat gentler than the brusque Father Butler of "An Encounter," develops "staring" eyes as the idleness of his students is revealed (*P* 292) and thus furnishes a moral case for Stephen: "Was that a sin for Father Arnall to be in a wax or was he allowed to get into a wax when the boys were idle because that made them study better or was he only letting on to be in a wax? It was because he was allowed because a priest would know what a sin was and would not do it. But if he did it one time by mistake what would he do to go to confession?" (*P* 292).

The case first propounds a simple sin, which Stephen would recognize from his little prayer book with its "Examination of Conscience," asking "Did I give way to anger?" or some such question. Or was the priest allowed to sin (Stephen recognizes being "in a wax" as a sin, as he makes clear in judging that it requires confession) if he had a good end in mind—to improve study? Thus enter the moral complexities of what means to a good end may be allowed. Then the possibility that the priest may be using duplicity, merely pretending anger in order to achieve his end. He decides the case in favor of the second answer, the special privilege Stephen bestows upon a priest. Since the priest would know (as a small boy might not until his confession booklet made it plain) what a sin was, he would not do it. Then somehow he must be allowed to commit this sin, and allowed no doubt on the basis of that good end of better study. Stephen's mind has thus simply and effectively set the stage for the "any means to an end" Jesuit that has slunk through English literature from *Macbeth* through *Henry Esmond* and beyond.

Stephen's process is convincing and most reasonable, mirroring the way in which the child grapples with the problems which confront him. Is Joyce's process equally simple, confined to the limited context in which the seven- or eight-year-old Stephen operates? The twenty-five-year-old family man could scarcely, like the child, conceive of Arnall's activity without including the crucial element which Stephen does not advert to—does Arnall operate in a context of love or of hate for the child? If Arnall does choose to get angry, does he do it on a sinful basis, ultimately hate, or does he do it, perhaps even mistakenly, on a basis of love? Stephen is no doubt struggling to some apprehension of that when he guesses, "because he was allowed." But the relatively mature and somewhat sophisticated Joyce could not in his own mind ingenuously leave it at that. Who allows, and on what basis?

Stephen is going to develop a distrust of his Jesuit masters, a growing dislike and a pressure to escape that he will compare, in *Stephen Hero* 142, to the flame and wind of Pentecost seeking release. Is Joyce the artist preparing for this, as he chooses to stress this element of Stephen's consciousness? Of course he is, but the basis for Joyce's own artistic choice also poses a question.

Is Joyce the artist planning and effecting his own personal revenge on the Jesuits? Or is he wholeheartedly devoting himself to the artistic end of expressing the human experience of a person who happens (or who chooses) to hate Jesuits—quite apart from the question of whether Jesuits are in themselves hateful or not? I see the matter more in that second light, though I am aware that Joyce's personal attitudes naturally have numerous influences, some apparent and most not. But as I observe the young Joyce moving from the straightforward narrative essay he wrote for *Dana* in January of 1904[3] through the opinionated intrusions of the superior commentator in *Stephen Hero* to the unobtrusive management of the relatively invisible commentator in *Portrait*, I conclude that Joyce the artist wants to concentrate on Stephen's own experience, without establishing whether Stephen's judgments about outside reality are right or wrong.

What counts in *Portrait* is how Jesuits, like other things, exist in Stephen, not how they exist in themselves. If they do use a bad means to a good end, that would be a blow aimed at real Jesuits, but, as I can make out the matter, no such thing is presented as certainly happening in *Portrait*. Father Dolan does hesitate when he finds that there is good reason for Stephen's inactivity, but he hits him anyway. Stephen's speculations about the moral implications of Father Arnall's getting red with anger have indeed set the stage for supposing that Father Dolan may like Pilate be agreeing that one boy must suffer injustice for the general good of discipline. But that is not stated in *Portrait,* as it doubtless would have been in *Stephen Hero.* And in that momentary hesitation, Dolan *may* have been establishing some kind of objective basis to justify his act. The condemnation of Dolan, even in Stephen, is not absolute. This strikes me as a vitally important critical point, since a book attacking the Jesuits would not, in Stephen's definition nor in mine, be literature, but didactic or moral or pornographic exhortation to act, not to contemplate. Stephen hates Jesuits, but even Stephen knows that his hatred does not really constitute reality outside himself. So does Joyce. Joyce aims to portray Stephen, and the Jesuits in the book serve that purpose.

The Jesuits emerge from the book as monstrous because in Stephen they are so. But even Stephen does not arrive at a fixed and certain ultimate judgment. As I can see Stephen's attitude, his rational conclusion is, "I don't like them, and I suspect they may be evil." His conclusion remains, more or less, a relative one, made in a Catholic environment where the basic assumption of at least theoretical operation of divine and human love is not absent, where Stephen remains aware of his own deficiencies and incertitudes, and where in youthful resentment and rebellion Stephen is constantly opposing fictional evil Jesuits to the real men whose ultimate motives he is in nonemotional moments aware he does not comprehend. As I can understand the nature of literature, it is essential that the mystery of free choice in the human spirit remain mysterious. If it is *comprehended,* as Theseus desires, then a human mind has encircled both man and God, and the result necessarily is abstract trash. If, as in some dramatizations of Joyce's work, the Jesuits are depicted as actually plotting and carrying through the humiliation of little Stephen, and the spiritual basis for that perversion is left to the bigotry of established anti-Jesuit tradition, the result is propaganda, not literature. In *Portrait,* far more than in *Stephen Hero,* the moral basis for the acts of the Jesuits, like that of humans in reality, remains mysterious. Thus *Portrait* emerges as literature (the same mystery of course remains for Stephen and all other human beings in the book) rather than as an illustrated anti-Catholic tract.

To return to the Clongowes schoolroom scene in *Portrait,* as soon as the question of Father Arnall's motive has been formed in Stephen's mind, Father Dolan, with the murky dramatic air of *Macbeth* hovering equivocally over him and promising endless "tomorrow's" of fear and threat and pain, introduces, with a serpentine swish of the soutane, a strong suspicion of evil motive. "Cruel and unfair" are the words that later echo in Stephen's battered and confused and resentful consciousness. As little Stephen looked up (in this perfectly imagined "point-of-view") and saw that "whitegrey not young face, his baldy whitegrey head with fluff at the sides of it," and above all the steel rims with the "no-coloured eyes" looking through, he was prepared for an evil attack. His second impression in the book (the first is in his ear) is of his father's eye through the monocle. Jesuit eyes will frighten and anger him from now on (Arnall's staring eyes were a mild source of fear). And Stephen, feeling the priestly fingers touch his hand to straighten it for the blow of the pandy-bat, is in no position to suppose that the priest may be doing this out of basic love; that the interrogation, to Stephen so brutal and impersonal, with the priest seemingly treating his name as something odd, might be intended as a concerned, if crude, effort to establish a basis for a just punishment; that the priest's assumption might be that Stephen, like Fleming, who prepared his hands for Dolan's attack, might be prepared to deal with him on some common ground of friendly brutality. Stephen cannot take any such possibilities about Dolan into consideration, but what about Joyce? If he too, as he wrote, chose to consider Dolan clearly a sadistic and brutal man, or a conniving monster torturing a child for a good end, he had to arrive at such certitude on grounds of hatred or of prejudice, not of rational conviction. It is reasonable and convincing that Stephen, caught in a frightening situation he could not comprehend or control, having been taught that God stood behind the priest and that the universe was governed by a fair and kind Providence, would conclude that Dolan must be evil. Joyce expresses the basis for that conclusion with concentrated power. He would in my judgment be a deficient artist if he agreed with it, and fitted his text to such agreement.

   The spiritual director, some eight or nine years later, speaks to the young Stephen, almost ready for the university (or the seminary), about his vocation. Now the entries concerning the Jesuits in Joyce's Trieste notebook begin to find their full expression.[4] The venality of speech between pastor and flock, to which Joyce refers, grows from the notion that the priests, like Simon Magus, will sell their freedom for power—a notion stressed, as we have seen, in "The Sisters." They will barter salvation to the flock in return for submission and, perhaps, money. The fingers of this priest, "deft" like most priestly fingers in Stephen's imagination, prepare a noose of language, sinuously controlled and manipulated to lead Stephen to an assent he barely escapes expressing. Stephen had heard again that ominous "swish of a soutane" (*P* 414), the hiss like those of the devils in Book Ten of *Paradise Lost*. The slow, deft fingers which he sees correspond to the "low discreet accent" which he hears, speaking "with soft design." As Stephen thinks that phrase and feels his face being searched by the eyes in the shadow, he sturdily but without conviction denies the suspicion that had come to him those years before in Father Arnall's classroom: "Whatever he had heard or read of the craft of jesuits he had put aside frankly as not borne out by his own experience. His masters, even when they had not attracted him, had seemed to him always intelligent and serious priests, athletic and high-spirited prefects. He thought of them as men who washed their bodies briskly with cold water and wore clean cold linen" (*P* 415). But "an unresting doubt flew hither and thither before his mind." Perhaps this cold water masked lustful devils, as the notebook entry "they are erotically preoccupied" implies. This "vital circumstance" may be the clue that Stephen had failed to perceive: "Some jesuits were walking round the cycletrack in the company of ladies. The echoes of certain expressions used in Clongowes sounded in remote caves of his mind" (*P* 417). The monsters he had been finding in his own Minotaurian caves may, he suspects, find their counterparts in the true venality of the jesuits he will not honor with capitalization. The "pride" so stressed in the fanatical praise of the "power" of the priesthood echoes in Stephen's response: "A flame began to flutter again on Stephen's cheek as he heard in this proud address an echo of his own proud musings. How often had he seen himself as a priest wielding calmly and humbly the awful power of which angels and saints stood in reverence! His soul had loved to muse in secret on this desire" (*P* 418).

The similarity of the diction in this whole scene to that in Hopkins's "The Windhover: to Christ our Lord" stresses the fact that the model for the spiritual director was in actuality a colleague of Hopkins, that the room was one where the visiting Hopkins could have spoken to young Irishmen not very many years before—maybe while Stephen was musing in Father Arnall's classroom twenty miles to the west (more or less). The Jesuit appeal to the power and mastery of knighthood operates in both contexts ("If ever he was impelled to cast sin from him and to repent, the impulse that moved him was the wish to be her knight" [*P* 357]). Hopkins urges his hiding heart to buckle on the armor of Christ's knight, in the dual contexts of Ignatius's Kingdom of Christ meditations and in Jesuit treatment of the Sacred Heart devotion.

> My heart in hiding
> Stirred for a bird,—the achieve of, the
>   mastery of the thing.
> Brute beauty and valour and act, oh, air, pride,
>   plume, here
> Buckle! AND the fire that breaks from thee then . . .

The fire (on its most literal level) is the divine fire pictured in devotional pictures of the Sacred Heart, symbol of the divine Pentecostal fire Christ shares with his members. The "pride" which corresponds to the bird's ecstatic "pride of place" and the knightly "plume" which symbolizes the mastery of the bird's wing both echo the Jesuit imagery of the *Deutschland*'s final lines: "Pride, rose, prince, hero of us, high priest,/Our hearts' charity's hearth's fire, our thoughts' chivalry's throng's Lord."

In the scene with the dean of studies, Joyce brings to a climax Stephen's carefully built portrait of the Jesuit as a complex, unattractive, and probably corrupt man. Almost all of the Trieste notebook items appear in these pages. The dean, modeled after Father Darlington, whose efforts to reveal the Catholicism in Shakespeare are noted in "Scylla and Charybdis" (*U* 205), illustrates the "nice terms of their philosophy," "levites," lack of love, exile from homeland and language, flattery, brisk and impartial dealing with the mob of students, and judging by categories rather than by existing reality or dynamic experience. The contrast of the angle of Stephen's vision in his fearful looking up at Father Dolan and his looking down on the dean takes on some symbolic significance as the grown and contemptuous college man looks down on the crouched figure.

That the dean, like Father Dolan, is for Stephen diabolical emerges from Joyce's description of the setting: "He opened the door of the theatre and halted in the chilly grey light that struggled through the dusty windows. A figure was crouching before the large grate and by its leanness and greyness he knew that it was the dean of studies lighting the fire" (*P* 448). The struggles of anemic light throughout Dubliners appears here, and the hellish atmosphere which opens "Ivy Day in the Committee Room" foreshadowed this Jesuit setting: "Old Jack raked the cinders together with a piece of cardboard and spread them judiciously over the whitening dome of coals. When the dome was thinly covered his face lapsed into darkness but, as he set himself to fan the fire again, his crouching shadow ascended the opposite wall and his face slowly re-emerged into light" (*D* 129). The tone of the dean's description is less poetic, but shares the chill, the lack of light, the crouching lean judicious figure.

The dean moves immediately into categories, "the liberal arts" and "the useful arts." Stephen observes, and arranges his own dislike and contempt for the dean into jesuitical categories of his own, based on his experience with Jesuits and Jesuit attitudes, liberally mixed with his responses to the anti-Jesuit tradition he has evidently probed with interest.

He provides four categories for the dean's "lowly service" (*P* 448): a) tending the fire upon the altar, b) bearing tidings secretly, c) waiting upon worldlings, d) striking swiftly when bidden. The last, of course, ties the dean closely to Father Dolan. Stephen muses on in elegant, almost lush biblical language, perceiving the absence in the dean of any light, beauty, or sweet "odour." And he arrives at his climactic insight, a vision of a Jesuit's will, given over wholly to obedience as a lover gives himself over to the act of love or a warrior to the thrust into his enemy: "a mortified will no more responsive to the thrill of its obedience than was to the thrill of love or combat his aging body, spare and sinewy, greyed with a silverpointed down" (*P* 449).

Stephen develops that treatment of the effect of the celebrated "blind obedience" on the Jesuit by quoting from and interpreting a bit the "Letter on Obedience" which Ignatius wrote to some restless scholastics, perhaps hoping through traditional rhetorical excess to move them to a slightly more tolerant attitude toward acknowledging some authority in their superior. Stephen, who knows this letter so well, could not well be ignorant of the principle underlying the letter as well as Catholic teaching in regard to the hell which so frightened Stephen in chapter 3—namely, the principle of infinite love. Neither hell nor Jesuit obedience can be in Catholic terms understood at all except on the presupposition that love is operative in both cases. If it is not, then both become perverse, "cruel and unfair," monstrous. There is little or no love in the retreat of chapter 3 or apparent in the detached dean of this scene, but we hear the retreat that Stephen heard, which is most probably not the one that emerged from Arnall's lips or the one that some boy not deaf to the love involved may have heard; we see the dean that Stephen sees, who differs from the dean that a student who loved that dean actually did see. Stephen chooses to respond to both on the grounds that the God who made hell is a threatening "dio boia" (*U* 213), analogous to Father Dolan, and that the Jesuit who agrees to obey his superior in all things (Stephen never quotes the next phrase, "where there appears no sin") as if he were literally giving over his will as a stick in an old man's hand, to be used any way at all, has made himself a zombie, a thing like a human programmed by space-creatures to bring the human race into submission.

Explanations of Catholic teaching on hell or the Jesuit vow of obedience were known to Stephen—he gives them a cold and patronizing glance in this scene with the dean—but for his own purposes he acts as if they do not exist. He does not seek to refute them; he ignores them. He projects into the dean that lack of love which years before he had more reasonably projected into Father Dolan. Then his fear and lack of sophistication prevented any reasoning beyond the means of escape from his predicament. Now he does have bases for questioning a construct based on hatred and fear, but he ignores those in favor of reasons suggesting that the Jesuit shares the evil of a Roman Catholic God who creates hell. The "nocoloured eyes" of Father Dolan have gained complexity but reveal in the dean the same hellish lack: "Stephen saw the silent soul of a jesuit look out at him from the pale loveless eyes" (*P* 449). Then he proceeds to speak of one influence on that silent soul, with repeated hissing adjectives that recall both the swish of the soutane and Milton's "subtlest beast of all the field": "Even the legendary craft of the company, a craft subtler and more secret than its fabled books of secret subtle wisdom, had not fired his soul with the energy of apostleship" (*P* 449–50).

There is here a significant shift revealing the deliberate duplicity behind Stephen's view. In his scene with the spiritual director, he claimed, "Whatever he had heard or read of the craft of jesuits he had put aside frankly as not borne out by his own experience" (*P* 415). Now he chooses to suppose that the same craft, now assumed to exist, had operated in the dean's soul. Some years have intervened, and it might possibly be argued that the university Jesuits had revealed more craft to him than had those at Belvedere, or that he himself is in a better intellectual position to perceive it, but even if so, Joyce gives no evidence of any such thing. The young man (whom Joyce once contrasted, by emphasizing "young," with himself) chooses condemnation for the Jesuit, and deliberately manipulates Jesuit expressions to justify even the extraordinary statement that this Jesuit acted with no love at all, without joy and without hatred of evil, but like a robot or a devil.

> It seemed as if he used the shifts and lore and cunning of the world, as bidden to do, for the greater glory of God, without joy in their handling or hatred of that in them which was evil but turning them, with a firm gesture of obedience, back upon themselves: and for all this silent service it seemed as if he loved not at all the master and little, if at all, the ends he served. *Similiter atque senis baculus,* he was, as the founder would have had him, like a staff in an old man's hand, to be left in a corner, to be leaned on in the road at nightfall or in stress of weather, to lie with a lady's nosegay on a garden seat, to be raised in menace. (*P* 450)

Those four activities illustrate, in Stephen's careful development, the four categories of service on the previous page, now specified in the stick: left in the corner while the fire is tended; leaned on as one delivers secret messages at all times and in all weathers; neglected as one tends a worldly lady; and to be raised like a pandybat in hellish threat.

The priest's face, like that of the spiritual director, where Stephen saw "a mirthless reflection of the sunken day" (*P* 421), here seems "an unlit lamp or a reflector hung in a false focus" (*P* 451). And what did it mask, something merely dull or a cloud charged with danger: "A dull torpor of the soul or the dullness of the thundercloud, charged with intellection and capable of the gloom of God?" (*P* 451). That image stems from Stephen's experience of a look from the "dark stern eyes" of the rector at Belvedere: "In the silence their dark fire kindled the dusk into a tawny glow. Stephen's heart had withered up like a flower of the desert that feels the simoom coming from afar" (*P* 360–61). Young Stephen, not too young to have found out and used the Nighttown facilities, reveals a sentimental concern, not altogether unlike the concerns of Gertie MacDowell, in his use of sweet Shelleyan images to express the threat to his vulnerable heart from the threatening Jesuit hellish fire. And the other extreme of supposedly divine love, after his confession, adds a drooling tone of oversweet piety: "and his prayers ascended to heaven from his purified heart like perfume streaming upwards from a heart of white rose" (*P* 404).

Stephen, as the dean challenges him on "tundish," takes, as well as he can, the stance of the elder brother of the prodigal. With some pity and with another shift on the "waiting on worldlings" category, Stephen coldly grants the Jesuits credit for the unfair judgment visited upon them by so many. Joyce himself could have thought of the ending of "Grace," where "the lax and the lukewarm and the prudent" (*P* 455) gather at the feet of Father Purdon, who there appears the most viciously worldly of all, perverting divine grace to crass toleration of mammon. But that is, after all, a parable, and here Stephen is dealing with his own judgments on men he hates, not, as he evidently judges, with total justice.

The surface change of tone, in regard to Jesuits, in the fifth chapter of *Portrait* can be quite dramatically demonstrated in Stephen's two imaginings of the activities of Jesuits. In his horrible nightmare during his Belvedere retreat (*P* 395), goatish creatures with human faces slaver out soft sibilant language, noiselessly issuing from grey lips like those of Father Dillon saying his office (*SH* 90). They reveal themselves quite clearly as the Jesuits Stephen knew at Clongowes and Belvedere. The "malice of evil glittered in their hard eyes," their "cruel malignity" accompanies their swishing, like "the swish of the sleeve of the soutane" (*P* 295) of the threatening Father Dolan. Like the pervert's words and thoughts in "An Encounter" (*D* 36), they move in slow, closing circles, like crushing walls in Gothic novels. The suggestion of lechery and perversion—"the hell reserved for his sins: stinking, bestial, malignant, a hell of lecherous goatish fiends" (*P* 395)—had been more pointedly and less artistically made by the narrative voice of *SH*: "The President gathered in his soutane for the ascent with a slow hermaphroditic gesture" (*SH* 98).

The *commedia dell' arte* tone of the Jesuits' goatish capering in Stephen's mind four years later, during his final months at the university, derives from Stephen's growing maturity, of course, but in part also from almost the only sympathetic relationship with a Jesuit in the book. Stephen obviously likes his Italian teacher, Father Charles Ghezzi, and admires in him the ability to mingle sorrow over Bruno and sensual delight in *risotto* (*P* 521). This uncharacteristic reaction in Stephen possibly results from the fact that Ghezzi, as a foreigner dealing with Stephen in a language which does not, like English, inhibit him, poses no Irish limiting threat. And any ecclesiastical threat he may embody, like that foreshadowed by the burning of Bruno, can be, like the minimal and not really serious threat of the very young Heron, Nash, and Boland, when they beat the "heretic" (*P* 330–31), easily peeled away. "The plump roundheaded professor of Italian with his rogue's eyes" (*P* 457) emerges last from "the limp priestly vestments" lining Stephen's mind. The growing absence of threat to his artistic self and the development of his own defenses and plans for escape are among the reasons that make it possible for Stephen, in chapter 5, to regard with contemptuous tolerance the "deep fast laughter . . . their rude malice . . . sudden dignity . . . whispering two and two behind their hands" (*P* 457) of the Jesuits. He is not involved; they are now "smacking one another behind." Father Ghezzi's behind gives a rare tone of likable humanity to the Jesuits of *Portrait,* and prepares both for "the salute of Almidano Artifoni's sturdy trousers" (*U* 255) at the end of "Wandering Rocks" and for a far more humane attitude toward Jesuits in *Ulysses.*

This new attitude focuses on two real Jesuits, the model for Father Purdon, Bernard Vaughan, S. J. (who joined the society in the group which included Gerard Hopkins), and John Conmee, S. J. (buried near Hopkins in Glasnevin). Stephen, "you fearful jesuit" (*U* 3), of course never loses the effects of the imagery and customs, nor the pressures of the doctrines and attitudes, which he experienced in his years with the Jesuits. But the two Jesuits in *Ulysses* are not seen exclusively through Stephen's consciousness but through the wider mind of a more sophisticated, far more tolerant, but still quite skeptical, observer. One great difference is that the observer in *Ulysses* can laugh, which poor Stephen, harried and egotistic, cannot easily do. Thus Father Conmee, with his meticulous habits, his carefully modulated judgments, his mild courtly snobbery, his quietly calculated use of people, his disingenuous blessing of sinners as he reads of quite different "Sin" in his breviary, his romantic and comfortably snobbish dreams of an honored courtly Don John in good old Catholic feudal days, his earnest trudging off on a charitable errand, can be a symbol of the Roman Power drawing the ecclesiastical arm of the great X formed by Church and State in "Wandering Rocks".[5] He provides a fairly attractive and somewhat funny symbol, quite different from any of those threatening-eyed Jesuits in *Portrait.*

Some critics, notably Marilyn French in her stimulating recent study of *Ulysses,* find Father Conmee calculating and, like the dean in *Portrait,* without love or feeling in his treatment of others.[6] Such opinion is based principally, I believe, not in Joyce's open-ended text but in the motives the critics project into Conmee's reaction to the sailor and his response to the death of so many innocents killed in the boat accident in New York. Bloom had pitied these last (*U* 182). Conmee seems to Miss French unfeeling and selfish: "Because he chooses to disregard the painful, Conmee finds it easy to accept and dismiss the sufferings of others" (p. 119). She notes the instances of Conmee's thinking "not too long" about soldiers and sailors having their legs shot off and what seems to her an unfeeling brief dismissal of the burned victims. The "not too long" may have nothing at all to do with the wounded man. It may be, as Joyce perhaps also knew from experience, a reaction to having thought far too many times about St. Ignatius's wounded leg in the battle at Pamplona, the occasion for his conversion and the composition of the *Spiritual Exercises.* And, on the other hand, Conmee's apparently clipped "still, an act of perfect contrition" (*U* 221), which in Miss French's indignant text breaks out with italics, may have, in Father Conmee's interior, all the emotional implications and profound, concerned love that emerge from Hopkins's *The Wreck of the Deutschland* and "The Loss of the

Eurydice." Both those Jesuits face the situation of sudden and painful death, and both, in their different modes of expression, take comfort in the possibility of a response to divine love even in the midst of that suffering. The act of perfect contrition, to them, is not the recitation of set words, but the climactic achievement of divine life. I do not know what Conmee's deep and ultimate response was. Nor does the narrative voice, whose clipped, amused, somewhat mocking tone probably indicates that the narrator doesn't much care. But the narrator does not specify the ultimate, callous selfishness that Miss French finds so detestable. He does, in fact, leave the mystery of ultimates among the unfacts where it belongs.

Bernard Benstock, in his satisfying evocation of the Ireland that emerges from Joyce's imagination, has one sentence that might seem to accord with Miss French's notion of Conmee, in regard to the revelation of Jesuit laughter over Stephen's attack on Dolan: "Yet several years later Mr. Dedalus reports to the family that Conmee had passed the matter off as a joke with Father Dolan and the other priests, a subtle betrayal of Stephen's trust in the kindly priest" (p. 37).[7] If one were to take this as a statement of fact in regard to Conmee's interior intention to betray Stephen, it would accord with Miss French's confident limitation of inaccessible reality. But Benstock, I believe, intends to focus on the reaction in Stephen. There surely Conmee's act is a betrayal. Stephen undoubtedly felt it so. In *SH* the narrative voice might have informed us that it was a betrayal. In *P* we are left with a silent space (*P* 320), where the feeling of Stephen will surely emerge in us. But there is room there too for Simon's crude, hearty admiration of diplomacy, and, if one finds it inside one, revulsion at the possibility or the likelihood of the betrayal of a child's innocent trust. That last I do not find. It perhaps takes a Jesuit like me to suspect that in the laughter of Father Conmee lurk both a commendation to Father Dolan (for whom Father Conmee would also have loving consideration) of his zeal to promote study and a cautionary rebuke to take care against offending both justice and the sensitivities of a child more vulnerable than the resin-hardened Fleming. But the open-ended text respects human mystery, and probably a sensible critic will do the same. Joyce's text leaves us precisely where reality outside ourselves (and inside too, for that matter) leaves us—unable with certitude to judge whether any given human is ultimately worthy of condemnation or of approval. We can of course guess, and it is sometimes fun to do that—and sometimes necessary. But if we insist that we have, in spite of the cloud of facts and unfacts we cannot reach or know, attained to objective certitude before which all must bow, then we truly are expository asses.

Bernard Vaughan, in whom Joyce took some interest not unmixed, I would guess, with some entertainment ("Fr. B. V. is the most diverting public figure in England at present. I never see his name but I expect some enormity" [*Letters,* 2:182]) introduces another fairly light touch to Joyce's treatment of actual Jesuits. Both Bloom and Conmee recall Vaughan's dramatic sermonizing (*U* 82 and 219), and Father Conmee thinks of his eyes which were to him (as they could never have been for Stephen) "droll." The cockney imitation which Conmee recalls fits perfectly with Hopkins's experiences with his fellow scholastic: "Mr. Vaughan took off Cornelius the philosopher's servant—'a-bullockin', ay and a-bullyraggin' teoo.' "⁸ I used to think that Joyce had slipped up in having Conmee think "Of good family too would one think it? Welsh, were they not?" (*U* 220). The easy humanistic tie-up with Henry Vaughan might well be a characteristic of Conmee's mind, and the lack of accuracy could be some indication of his competence as a historian. But it seems incredible to me that Conmee, one year after the death of Bernard's celebrated brother, the leading prelate in the Catholic church in England, whose majestic sarcophagus lies in the somewhat Oriental cathedral he built in London, would not have shared the knowledge of every other contemporary literate Catholic about the Vaughan family, and never have imputed what to that English family, even from the west of England, would surely seem a "foreign" taint. Still, as I have thought about it, it might be a way for Conmee, who must have experienced with his English brethren many a slight about his Irish blood and accent, to make for his own diversion a trifling dig at the chauvinism of the English—so strikingly evident in Hopkins during his own "exile" among the Irish. Even if it was a "mistake," it can be a "portal of discovery." In any case, it seems to me that Joyce shows a good deal of affection for John Conmee, who indeed did for Joyce and his family many favors.

The mature Joyce certainly managed to be funny about the founder of the Jesuits. Joyce saw himself as like Ignatius in several ways. Brought up as he was, he would most naturally use the tradition in which he developed as a source for his images of the artist as priest, as Christ, as victim, as divine Word, as Creator. It is reasonable to suppose that his mother, like Stephen's mother, passionately desired him to be a priest. In Stephen's case, this appears, as Schutte points out, in the various ruses May uses to hold him under her influence, most likely based in some measure on Joyce's experiences with his own mother.⁹ On this basis one can understand May's hostility even to the Jesuit university, since she wanted Stephen at Maynooth preparing formally for the priesthood.

Joyce well knew that Ignatius had written a book that swept the world, particularly his own Dublin and Jesuit world, *The Spiritual Exercises,* upon which Hopkins was basing his own poetic vision across town while Joyce was growing up surrounded by the same words and images. He wanted like Ignatius to be a knight of the Blessed Virgin, and like Hopkins's Perseus or Windhover, to buckle on the Pauline armor of Christianity and destroy the dragon or the Minotaur or soar like the hawk (Hopkins and Joyce both favored Greek and avian images for their expressions of faith). Joyce shifted considerably as he developed, beginning to identify with the virgin-devouring Minotaur and to humanize his hawk into Icarus, but the influence of Ignatius did not leave him. He continued to operate with the controlled imagination setting up the Composition of Place (or at least he remembered that he had trained in that school), he admired the power of Ignatian writing and retained his respect for the effectiveness of Jesuit "cunning," and he took to himself the command of Ignatius, based on Christ's "I am come to cast fire on the earth" ([Luke 12:9] operative in "The Windhover: to Christ our Lord"), that his followers should go forth and set the world on fire. Thackeray could have worked this out for Father Holt in terms of arson; Joyce like Stephen Hero thinks at once, with Cranly, of Pentecostal flame of love and wisdom, expressed in tongues (*SH* 142).

Stephen's prayer to Ignatius ["Scylla and Charybdis," *U* 188], formed in the context of the armed vision of the dead king, in actuality an actor made up like Stephen himself in "the castoff mail of a court buck," reflects one Jesuit influence that Hopkins and Joyce both profited from—the intense concentration on the importance of imagination in prayer as well as in rhetorical endeavor, including creative literary art. The insistence on dealing with the concrete, the existing, the real helped to avoid getting lost in the abstractions of the theologians as of the poetasters. Louis L. Martz's study of the influence of Ignatian methods, *The Poetry of Meditation* (Yale, 1954), gives a wealth of background to such considerations. Stephen Hero, like the Stephen of *Ulysses*, aims "to acknowledge one's own humanity!" (*SH* 142). His dialog with Cranly has the tonality and repetition of a vacuous television ad for "gasid indigestion."

> —You mustn't think I rhapsodise: I am
> quite serious. I speak from my soul.
> —Soul?
> —Yes: from my soul, my spiritual nature.
> Life is not a yawn.

Life in Shaun does turn into a Yawn in the mature Joyce, and Shem's soul finds a new and lasting body in ink like the caustic dyes of the *Book of Kells*, sinking into lasting skin, carrying words even more lasting and incendiary than those of Ignatius through time and space, scattering the sparks of human, not divine, experience. The degraded echo of the Ignatian aim in Dublin we find in Ignatius Gallaher, in "A Little Cloud" and in *Ulysses*. "The Great Gallaher," as the "Aeolus" headline announced him (*U* 135), had waltzed on Sunday morning (*U* 88) as Ignatius had danced to cheer up Ortiz;[10] he had said that he would set out to paralyse Europe, more fitting to a *Dubliners* character than going forth to set Europe on fire (*U* 135); and he does maliciously exercise the cunning that he has, expressed in *Ulysses* as "the smartest piece of journalism ever known" (*U* 136), in attempting to crush and diminish Little Chandler in "A Little Cloud." Joyce did not lightly name him Ignatius.

Joyce adverts directly to Ignatius's fire image in *FW* 432–33. Ignatius had attempted to found a missionary order, to sail over the seas and bring the fire of divine love to humans separated by space from the Church of Christ. His command to spread that fire was addressed to Francis Xavier as that extraordinary man set off for the Orient. In *FW*, Jaun's eyes scan all the saints in the calendar before he chooses: "From the common for ignitious Purpalume to the proper of Francisco Ultramare, last of scorchers" (*FW* 432–33). The "proper" and the "common" refer to the classification of prayers for the masses. The "common" will refer to a class, as the Confessors or the Evangelists. The "proper" refers to prayers or a prayer designated for specific individuals. Joyce, I take it, makes an adjective out of the uncapitalized "ignitious," literally full of fire, and makes a class out of the "Purpalume," as it were the Evangelists or the Writers of Purple Prose or the "blushfed porporates" of the Vatican on *FW* 185. Juan's mass, then, celebrates Pentecostal Literary Artists with Jesuit backgrounds in general, and in particular, the proper prayer is addressed to the most famous of modern missionaries, Francis Xavier, S. J., who also "winged away on a wildgoup's chase across the kathartic ocean" (*FW* 185). The purple pen derives, like the "penisolate" of the opening page of *FW*, from the mixture of military and artistic sources for the words. Father Arnall's purple echoes of seventeenth-century Jesuit prose can provide the color, and the plume of the knight (also featured in "The Windhover: to Christ our Lord") merges with the pen of the artist. The mixture of the crusade of Christian Soldiers with Shem's own artistic campaign can be seen in the words that end the paragraph, a parody of the liturgical formula for citing a scriptural text: "Words taken in triumph, my sweet assistance, from the sufferant pen of our jocosus inkerman militant of the reed behind the ear" (*FW* 433).

I find Joyce imitating Ignatius more directly, by founding a religious order of his own. In the course of "The Mime of Mick, Nick, and the Maggies," we come to the lovely religious passage in which the animals, like the children, prepare for sleep, mostly in terms of Catholic and Jewish holidays. Among these animals are the fish in the Liffey: "And now with robby brerfox's fishy fable lissaned out, the threads simwhat toran and knots in its antargumends, the pesciolines in Liffeyetta's bowl have stopped squiggling about Junoh and the whalk and feriaquintaism and pebble infinibility and the poissission of the hoghly course" (*FW* 245). These Pesciolines, with all their Jewish and Mohammedan connections, are clearly enough, judging from what they have been squiggling about, a Catholic order like the Ursulines not very far from the Liffey. They have listened to the Scriptures, maybe the whole thing (Simhat Torah, the Joy in the Law, celebrating the year's reading of the whole law, here mixed a bit with the more modern Koran) with help from the

Targum in dealing with loose threads and argumentative knots. We perceive that these Pesciolines are seminarians, and they have studied four courses during the day, two in the morning and two in the afternoon with a bit of free time for dipping into the beast fables with "that wrynecky fix . . . in the beast circuls" (*FW* 480) or into religious history (recalling the Reverend Love in "Wandering Rocks" suspected of a "new gunpowder plot" by O'Molloy [*U* 231]) with "the depleted whilom Breyfawkes as he had entered into an ancient moratorium, dating back to the times of the early barters" (*FW* 574-75).

In the morning the Pesciolines had studied Scripture and the sacraments. In their scripture course they had discussed Jonas and the whale, though apparently the discussion had wandered a bit into some treatment of the queen of the gods and perhaps something of the wanderings of Ulysses on the whale-walks. They were dealing with the Eucharist, evidently, in the course on the sacraments, since Feria Quinta will refer to the Thursday that counts most of all for Catholic theologians, the Thursday of the Last Supper. This would of course be a touchy subject for Catholic fish, particularly no doubt for Dublin fish, since no meat would pass Catholic lips on Friday. Anxiety would mix with Christian piety to wear down the energies of these involved students. In the course on the Church, the limits of papal power, and the limits of authority on the bed of the Liffey, rather than the more abstruse questions of papal infallibility, took up their attention. And the climactic course of the day, on the Trinity, dealing on this day with the Procession of the Holy Ghost, mixed in the food interests of Catholics and Jews, fish and hogs. No wonder the weary little fellows collapsed, so that not a flip-flap could be heard in all unwaking Finnyland. Joyce as founder reveals a loving Ignatian concern for his order.

And Joyce can be funny about Jesuits as seen through Buck Mulligan's eyes, self-centered like Stephen's, but with no saving real concern for literature, for the beauty of the word. Buck, not a totally reliable judge, tells Haines in "Wandering Rocks" that Stephen can never be a poet, since the Jesuits had driven his wits astray with visions of hell. He cannot warble the note of Swinburne, Buck judges, a poet also admired by Little Chandler. And as they emerge from the maternity hospital, Buck, as he did on the first page, calls Stephen a "jesuit," there an un-Siegfriedian fearful one, here with three other qualities, "Jesified orchidised polycimical jesuit!" (*U* 425). "Orchidised" refers to the sterility Buck judges that the Jesuit spirituality has inflicted on whatever natural Hellenistic drives Stephen might have had. "Polycimical" refers to the dirty personal habits of Stephen, and perhaps is influenced by remarks Stephen might have made similar to his musings on his mother's hands bloodied with her children's lice (*U* 10) or his more profound comparison of his lice and his thoughts, both "born of the sweat of sloth," in *P* 504. Maybe Stephen shared Joyce's own tendency to link lice with Jesuits, as in his letter to Stanislaus from Rome, 12 September 1906, in which he refers to Jesuits as "black lice," and Buck might have noted the tendency. "Jesified" I take to mean that the Jesuits had made Stephen into a Joking Jesus type, as Gogarty expressed in the original of the poem attributed to Buck in *Ulysses,* found in *Letters,* 2:127. Like Stephen, and somewhat like Joyce as seen by Gogarty, Joking Jesus doesn't swim; doesn't bathe; depends on others for support; breezily soars into the air; makes water into wine and then makes water for the seekers of free drinks (a foreshadowing of Shem's eucharistic caustic ink); throws dust in their eyes to make the blind see (as Christ spat on earth to put on the the eyes of the blind man); walked on water to avoid a bath; like Christ, owed his triumphal entry to an ass; left a sheep naked, like the priests of *Lycidas;* gets power by making men wretched through the confession box, forcing them, like Heron with Stephen, to "admit" they are sinners. The eucharistic lampooning so favored by Gogarty and by Buck, as in the Mother Grogan story (*U* 12), where the tea as Hellenic eucharist foreshadows Molly's eucharistic pot of blood and urine, so perceptively celebrated by Ellmann in *Ulysses on the Liffey,*[11] also ties up with the Christy story of the *Portrait*'s Christmas dinner (*P* 270), based on the story of a plasterer, looking for a place to relieve himself, mistaking his fellow workers' bucket of beer for a portable urinal, and also ties in with Edward the Seventh foreshadowing the black mass of Buck by appearing with "a plasterer's bucket on which is printed: Defense d'uriner," (*U* 590) and going on to sing with a "soft contentment" (which accords with Christy's "soft mouth" of *P* 270) of "Drinking whiskey, beer, and wine!" (*U* 594). Buck's aim certainly is to degrade the sacraments and the Jesuits, both doctrinally despised by him. This is not Stephen's aim, however. Stephen does indeed reject and despise Jesuits and sacraments, but not in the simple rational fashion of Buck. Like his relationship with the Temptress of the Villanelle, Stephen also loves and is fascinated by the beauty and by the celebration of life in the positive aspects of the Catholic vision, and he uses these, as he uses the Madonna, to suggest some nonbestial elements of human experience that are unavailable to the complacent scientific Buck. Stephen develops toward Shem, who makes no exclusively positive and absolute statements, while Buck foreshadows Shaun, whose favorite predications are "This exists that is it" (*FW* 186), not realizing, space creature that he is, that "one who deeper thinks will always bear in the baccbuccus of his mind that this downright there you are and there it is is only all in his eye" (*FW* 118).

The Stephen of *Stephen Hero* had much more of Buck and of Shaun in him, as I can hear the matter, than does the Stephen of *Portrait* and certainly of *Ulysses.* Stephen Hero freely condemned Jesuit influence and life: "The toy life which the Jesuits permit these docile young men to live is that I call a stationary march. The marionette life which the Jesuit himself lives as a dispenser of illumination and rectitude is another variety of the stationary march" (*SH* 187). The view of Jesuits in *Portrait* emerges not as a doctrinal statement but as the feeling and fear and rebellion inside Stephen. In *Stephen Hero* the Ignatian method of marking down one's progress in perfection is stated abstractly by Stephen Hero: "Kindly remember the minute bylaws they have for estimating the exact amount of salvation in any good work—what an Aristotelian invention!" (*SH* 187). In *Portrait* that proposition comes to far more effective life inside the seemingly renewed Stephen, who is actually operating on a diabolically selfish effort to grab power through apparent submission: "His life seemed to have drawn near to eternity; every thought, word and deed, every instance of consciousness could be made to revibrate radiantly in heaven: and at times his sense of such immediate repercussion was so lively that he seemed to feel his soul in devotion pressing like fingers the keyboard of a great cash register and to see the amount of his purchase start forth immediately in heaven, not as a number but as a frail column of incense or as a slender flower" (*P* 406).

The shift from the specious objectivity of *Stephen Hero* to the more artistically subjective *Portrait* is beautifully illustrated in the reversal of roles for Stephen and Cranly in their religious discussion, climactic in *Portrait*. We have already considered the Pentecostal imagery in the flame and the wind Stephen Hero feels within him, and the feeling springs most strongly from complex hidden sources as a response to Cranly's question, "Why are you so impatient with the Jesuits?" (*SH* 142). It is escape, Stephen says, that excites him, and he goes on to assert, as the Stephen of *Ulysses* does in "Oxen of the Sun," that the artist is better than Jesus, that the artists using Aquinas and Aristotle have made the Church the powerful and beautiful thing that she is. Stephen meets Cranly's ineffective defense of Christ's Church with silence. The "Stephen did not answer" of *SH* 142 becomes the climactic "Cranly did not answer" of *P* 520. The focus has shifted altogether to Stephen's interior. The reaction to the Jesuits has moved from the abstract body of mechanical men to the piggishness of the Jesuit whose young eyes had looked down on Stephen at Clongowes and whose name Joyce adopted at his confirmation (*Ellmann*, p. 29 and *P* 301, 513). The Swinburnian sad and solitary Jesus conjured up by Stephen Hero shifts in *Portrait* to the bravely solitary Stephen, content to endure hell in the service of his art. It is obvious to me, looking from my own Catholic angle (which I take in this instance to be also Joyce's), that Cranly, in speaking of that "noblest and truest friend," is speaking of the Christ of Catholicism, who alone could be described in such terms by Paul and by Hopkins and by honest John Byrne, the model for Cranly. As I see it, this is obvious to Stephen too, and his hesitation over the "seemed to have struck" reveals his own inner incertitude and discomfort as he applies to Cranly the "cold sadness" which Stephen Hero had found in Christ. It is on this basis, not on any homosexual impulse which he thinks might actually exist in Cranly, that Stephen turns for comforting rationalization to the question which shows Cranly that Stephen will not honestly face the ultimate confrontation. Cranly knows that Stephen knows of whom he is speaking, and thus Cranly realizes that attempts to communicate with Stephen are futile. Appropriately, Stephen goes at once into his diary, which is in this aspect an apt symbol of the hell which James Duffy had found in Phoenix Park, the deliberate choice of being alone.

That marionette image for the Jesuits, quoted above from *SH* 187, undergoes a somewhat similar transformation in *Ulysses,* shifting from the priests to the artist. Buck holds out to Stephen his Ursuline mirror (*U* 6) and quotes from Wilde's preface to *Dorian* to mock Stephen's bitterness at actually seeing his frustrated and insecure face, a thing Buck could not have done if it were a Wildean mirror, which, as Wilde argues in his "Intentions" essays, quoted later by Mr. Best and paraphrased by Stephen, does not reflect but determines. It is a Matthew Arnold objective mirror which Buck presents, and seems to show, according to its schizoid cracked abilities, the object as in itself it really is. The magic mirror of Bella Cohen, in "Circe" (*U* 567), achieves the Wildean ideal of showing the object as in itself it is not. Stephen and Bloom, gazing in the mirror, see the beardless and paralyzed face of Shakespeare crowned with cuckold's horns. Both of them have suffered usurpation, artistic and marital, and both are determined in their very being by Joyce's grasp of Shakespeare. Shakespeare is a dummy, as he reveals by speaking in dignified ventriloquy, and the voice is that of Joyce, operating under and in his ink as Christ operates in the Eucharist. Budgen explains the basis for Joyce's seeing Bloom as cuckold, and Stephen in "Scylla and Charybdis" has set forth the necessary basis in the artist's own experience for the mysterious existence of his characters in ink.[12] The ventriloquist is the invisible Joyce, and from the beardless Shakespeare, more closely tied to Stephen than to Bloom, there is an easy shift of dummies to the bearded face of Martin Cunningham, who looked like Shakespeare in "Grace" and whom Bloom, grateful for the kindness to his suicide father, saw as "Like Shakespeare's face" in "Hades" (*U* 96). Martin takes Bloom's joke about Dodd away from him in the carriage, and had thus already superimposed his voice on Bloom's. Now as an usurped husband he mirrors forth Bloom, and suggests some of the complications in the looking-glass world of the artist's imagination. In this complication of the marionette image, Joyce is the sole master and the only voice, and the magic mirror of his art does not really show the age what it is, but shows himself to himself. If we choose to join in, we need not be surprised if we do not see ourselves in Joyce's mirror as we are in ourselves, but find ourselves transformed into the grinning Irish grief-lined face of Joyce, and hear our voices in musical Irish lilt expressing the mystery we feel flowing through us.

Different people, however, hear different things. The model for Cranly, J. F. Byrne, did not at all like the treatment of Father Darlington in *Portrait*. When he was visiting Joyce in Paris in 1927, he objected particularly to the impression that "Joyce was venting his spleen on Father Darlington."[13] Joyce amiably agreed, "saying he was sorry he had written it as he had, and that he was sorry for certain other things he had written." Joyce knew how to treat a guest, but I gather that in some ways he meant what he said. I speculate that if he had, in the early years of the century, any particular animus against Father Darlington, that had faded. In any case, he knew that Byrne loved and respected Darlington, and he accepted that. And he would not be much interested in explaining to Byrne that the large attack on the Jesuits in *Portrait* was an essential element in the overserious, vulnerable, self-centered subject of his portrait—filled with hates and loves conflicting and competing and never neatly sorted into rational categories.

Budgen, a friend who developed an informed view of the mature artist, perceived the way in which Joyce dealt with his personal feeling about the Church and the Jesuits. Budgen makes a statement which seems especially valuable for getting my present problem into perspective. In a context which reveals, among other things, Joyce's profound interest in Catholic dogma, particularly the doctrine of the Trinity, Budgen says—

> The Holy Roman Catholic Apostolic Church in its Irish form was a net he had flown by, but having won the freedom he needed, he could admire the Church as an institution going on its own way unperturbed in obedience to the law of its own being . . . Joyce's attitude toward the Christian religion was twofold. When he remembered his own youthful conflict with it in its Irish-Roman form he could be bitterly hostile, but in general, viewing it as a whole as an objective reality and as epitomized human experience, and from a position well out of reach of any church's authority and sanctions it was for him a rich mine of material for the construction of his own myth. Then he was a collector displaying all a collector's ardor, as in the case of the *altkatholische Kirche* referred to above.[14]

The complexities of Joyce's inner responses to his own experiences with Catholicism certainly evade my own rational comprehension. But in the limited apprehension that I do have, I cannot find a solid foundation for the critical conviction that Joyce was wholeheartedly pro-Catholic or anti-Catholic. As far as his work is concerned, he seems to me to be neither. And one may suppose, too, that the "freedom" of which Budgen speaks, though not in regard to Catholicism but with careful distinction in relation to an "Irish-Roman form," is not simply freedom from Catholicism, necessarily, but freedom from restrictions which may have come, not from family and language and nation and church, but from the abuses of those things in themselves good. Joyce, at least as a young man, seemed to think he might be the occasion for improving conditions for his race, presumably so that something good which had been degraded or crushed might reassert itself. I do not, by the way, suppose that even as a young Romantic he ever took that moral notion as seriously as Shelley did, and I think also that he recovered from it fully before he completed his greatest final epic, but not at all because he hated or condemned or attacked Catholicism or Catholic doctrine.

This change is reflected in Joyce's late use of Hopkins's poems, a reaction I will discuss in the next chapter. If Joyce had quoted Hopkins in 1909, one would expect a heavy irony to encompass the use of the material. But his use of Hopkins some thirty years later seems to me quite a different story. I doubt that his basic rejection of Catholic principles changed much, if any, but I believe that I perceive a far more mellow toleration of Hopkins's own use of the Catholic dream, and a willingness to conceive of himself, without the acid and bitter reaction characteristic of the lonely Stephen, as sharing in some aura at least of supernatural Pauline optimism.

Hopkins had paraphrased Newman—"Did you ever see one?"[15]—using a passage of interest both to Jesuits and Jesuit haters in his effort to bring Bridges to examine his own anti-Jesuit feelings. Joyce had, certainly, seen a good many Jesuits, and he came up, unlike Byrne, with anti-Jesuit feelings, more virulent than Bridges's—but not so simple. Like Joyce's feelings about his mother and about Ireland, his feelings about Jesuits seem to me accompanied by guilt, suggested in Stephen's cold recital of the lack of justice in the attacks on Jesuits, and possibly echoed in reality by such comments as those Joyce made to Byrne. He was not, like Bridges, complacently condemning something he well knew to be altogether undesirable. And his artistic effort to express this human experience—i.e., of hating something that if you were objective, or if you allowed yourself to be deceived, or seduced, you might love—produces great literature. In that literature, however, condemnatory of the Jesuits as the early expression of it clearly is, I do not find any objective attack on the Jesuits by Joyce, any more than I find in Shylock any attack by Shakespeare on the Jews.

Readers and critics may use the *Portrait* to denigrate nonfictional Jesuits (as some have), but they do that on their own. In his shift from *Stephen Hero* to *Portrait,* Joyce took considerable pains not to do it, and at least in my reading largely succeeded. And nobody uses *Ulysses* or, above all, *Finnegans Wake* as any example of attack on real Jesuits or (with some few exceptions stemming from Stephen in *Ulysses*) on the Catholic church. The "cunning" of Shem and the priestly posturings of Shaun are always surrounded by laughter in *FW,* and neither lust nor fanaticism can survive laughter.

Some critics have found in the Porter scene in *Macbeth* a reflection of Shakespeare's perceptive distrust of real equivocating Jesuits. Shakespeare is operating in the dramatic mode, as Stephen conceived it. He depicts indeed the attitudes of his characters, but obviously those are not necessarily his. No sensible person attempts to establish Shakespeare's personal attitudes by attributing to him every attitude expressed by his characters. Stephen in "Scylla and Charybdis" does something close to that, but he doesn't do it with total seriousness. He does, however, reveal a good deal about his own imagination in his interpretation of Shakespeare's response to Jews and to Jesuits. In Shylock, Shakespeare expresses, according to Stephen, the situation involved in the Elizabethan "jewbaiting that followed the hanging and quartering of the queen's leech Lopez, his jew's heart being plucked forth while the sheeny was yet alive" (*U* 204). "Warkwickshire jesuits are tried and we have a porter's theory of equivocation" (*U* 205). Jesuits and Jews, I believe, tend to suggest each other in Stephen's imagination (even more in Joyce's), and sometimes, as here, in regard to the heart. I suspect that the Jewish heart which was the object of special devotion for the Jesuits and which confronted Stephen (and Joyce) in his home, in friends' homes, in his school, in churches and chapels, in Glasnevin cemetery, in his streets and country roads and shrines, has a reflection in that "jew's heart" of the Shylock discussion. Eglinton invites Stephen to prove that Shakespeare was a Jew, as Stephen's Jesuit dean had argued that Shakespeare was a Catholic (*U* 205). Bloom and Stephen, representative of the Old Law and the New Testament, the Jew and the Christian, the Hebrew and the Celt, both, in Circe's magic mirror, become aspects of the myriad-minded Shakespeare (*U* 567-68)— who is himself there the dummy aspect of the ventriloquist Joyce. And in *FW* Shem brings the relationships of Jew and Jesuit into unity when he "went into the society of jewses" (*FW* 423).

Joyce's heart imagery becomes more and more theologically profound, it seems to me, as Joyce matured. I will discuss this in some detail in my next chapter, though the matter is too complex and profound to submit easily to rational analysis. I will try to indicate the areas in which I suspect its presence, and leave it to the individual consciousness of each reader to see it or not. The situation is something like that which exists in discussion of Hopkins's "The Windhover: to Christ our Lord." In that sonnet the involvement of the devotion to the heart of Christ seems to me, now, obvious, but not so for most others, apparently. For me, the fire breaking from the heart would, even in the abstract, most naturally suggest Hopkins's interest in the central Jesuit devotion, evidenced most powerfully in his own magnificent sermon on the Sacred Heart. In a context of medieval and military contest (minion, dauphin, chevalier), of "catching" in the mind (the penetration of reality, the response of memory, understanding, and will), the situation seems obviously drawn from the meditation on Christ's kingdom in the *Spiritual Exercises* and obviously the same as that in the *Deutschland*:

> I whirled out wings that spell
> And fled with a fling of the heart to the heart of the Host.
> My heart, but you were dovewinged, I can tell,
> Carrier-witted, I am bold to boast,
> To flash from the flame to the flame then . . .
>
> (Stanza 3)

And the symbols with which "The Windhover" ends, both of them drawn from Christ's own treatment of his labor and passion—the plough from which the Christian does not take his hand and the ember cast to the ground to start many fires—find a subtle meeting point in the spears' being beaten into ploughshares. It is a spear that pierces Christ's heart and releases the gold red flood of divine life into time and space, and it is a ploughshare that as a result of its labor reflects the light of the world. Those symbols formed themselves for centuries around the devotion to Christ's passion, in Ireland from the spear piercing Christ's side on the High Crosses of Kells to the cry of Stephen's mother in "Circe" (*U* 582), and came into sharp focus in the modern liturgical expression of devotion to the Sacred Heart—

> Versicle: Take my yoke upon you, and learn of me.
> Response: Because I am meek and humble of heart.
> Antiphon for the Magnificat: I have come to cast fire upon the earth, and what do I wish but that it be kindled.[16]

I believe that there is evidence in the text of *Finnegans Wake,* as I will suggest in the next chapter, that Joyce in his maturity does allow himself to acknowledge some aspects of Hopkins's positive and profound expression of Jesuit love.

From the Catholic and Jesuit milieu in which he developed, Joyce drew many insights and attitudes and images which he shared with Hopkins, who not only shared that milieu but, I suspect, had some formative influence on the atmosphere Joyce found in University College. Compare the backgrounds of the quality "felt by the artist when the esthetic image is first conceived in his imagination" (*P* 481), and the backgrounds of Hopkins's expression in sexual terms of the male penetration of reality into the imagination, "The fine delight that fathers thought" (*Poems* 76, "To R. B."). An identical epistemological base lies beneath those images, the imagination imaged as a fertilizable ovum awaiting the sperm of some other existing being, that union resulting not in a child but in a word or a poem. Stephen's "conceived in his imagination" is identical with Hopkins's "leaves yet the mind a mother of immortal song," though the "jejune jesuit" carries it in his villanelle production into the religious sphere of the Incarnation, while the actual Jesuit treats it in a vividly imagined context of human coition.

The Joyce who could create, in "Oxen of the Sun," the powerful analogy between the organic development of language and the development of the child in the womb would surely respond with delight to Hopkins's image of the poem, in "To R. B.," as a child formed by mysterious and suprarational laws inside the womb of the mind. Stephen's "the luminous silent stasis of esthetic pleasure" (*P* 481) is drawn from the same metaphysical source as Hopkins's insight into the dynamic infinite beauty of God, beyond pieing: "whose beauty is past change: / Praise him" (*Poems* 37, "Pied Beauty").

On a theological plane, Joyce and Hopkins both use, in Augustinian context, the mystery of the Trinity as a base for dealing with the artist's generation of his word (and of his poem) and with his love for his word (and his aching desire for the poem which, as cosmic eunuch for love of Christ [cf. Matt. 19:12]—"birds build—but not I build; no, but strain, / Time's eunuch, and not breed one work that wakes" [Poems 74]—Hopkins cannot breed). The powers of the soul (memory, understanding, and will) reflect, in this context, the Father's generating expression of Himself in the Word, and their mutual spiration of infinite love in the Spirit. The human soul knows itself, not directly, but in knowing another, in generating its word. Thus in the formation of that word which expresses knowledge of another, the human soul knows and loves itself. Stephen, in seizing the Ballast Office clock (like Hopkins "catching" the windhover) is suffused with the beauty of his own soul in its act of knowing, experiencing *claritas,* and rests in the loving contemplation of himself epiphanized in seizing the clock (or any other being which surrenders itself to him). Thus the artist's aim is to express his own beauty, known and loved within the artist's own being, a finite reflection of the infinite act of God knowing and loving Himself. It is precisely the desolating absence of such interior experience of union with the Word that gives such depth to the concluding flat "explanation" of Hopkins's "winter world."

The mystery of the Incarnation finds marvelous expression in both artists. Hopkins writes of it in lyrical mode (to use Stephen's categories), and Joyce in dramatic. That is, Hopkins writes of it as a personal experience in himself, the seeing a reflection of Christ's infinite beauty in the limited beauty of the bluebell or of the windhover. Joyce writes of it as an analogy, the doctrine of infinite beauty enfleshed serving him as an image of finding his own human beauty perfectly expressed in the known beauty of the wading girl, partially expressed in the friend of *Chamber Music* (that shadowy male figure), in friends like Cranly and Mulligan. In *Ulysses,* I believe that Joyce finds the expression of human beauty partial in Stephen and in Bloom, greater in Bleephan and Stoom, greater yet in Molly, greatest in all three, the Trinitarian experience of human *claritas.* In *Finnegans Wake,* the Dreamer (who, among other possibilities, may be Joyce, may be the reader, or in eucharistic union, may be an identification of Joyce and his reader) contemplates enchantedly his or her beauty in wording and loving everything and everybody that he or she can apprehend.

"The enchantment of the heart" means a cardiac condition to Galvani (*P* 481). Stephen's mother sends him forth with the prayer that in exile he may learn "what the heart is and what it feels" (*P* 526). The Jesuitical context of "heart," so powerfully expressed by Hopkins, so deeply involved in the prayer on May Dedalus's lips, rouses itself with a new strange life, at least in my own reading, in Joyce's final magnificent lyrical, dramatic epic. There is a sea change, indeed, but my ear picks up, weaving through the skeptical and sardonic tone, priestly elements in the prayer which closes chapter 9 of *FW*. As young Joyce knew well from almost daily experience in Jesuit chapels, Jesuits pray to God to have mercy on us, to incline our hearts to love of God. The Joycean artist, writing from "the bowels of his misery" (*FW* 185), before he appeals to the vowels which bring him life and lasting being ("Ha he hi ho hu") and the sacred Eastern silence which expresses ultimate mystery ("Mummum"), misericordially prays: "Loud, heap miseries upon us yet entwine our arts with laughters low!" (*FW* 259).

6 Joyce and Hopkins

Joyce pictures Stephen thinking of himself as a member of the Society of Jesus, "The Reverend Stephen Dedalus, S. J." (*P* 422). Joyce has Shaun describe Shem's catching "europicolas" and, as we have seen, entering "the society of jewses" (*FW* 423). But so resonant was the "Non serviam" of Stephen (and apparently of the youthful Joyce) to the religion in which he spent his formative years that any comparison of Stephen, after his determination to reject Catholicism, to one who, like Hopkins, "did say *yes,*" would surely become mainly contrast.

Joyce himself, however, after suggesting in his pages many sometimes bitter, sometimes humorous contrasts between himself and Jesuits, does, as it seems to me, in the final chapter of his greatest book, hint at at least some comparison between HCE and Hopkins. Into his preparations for the coming dawn and resurrection of Finnegan, "om this warful dune's battam," Joyce introduces an echo of Hopkins's massive sonnet, a celebration of the resurrection of Christ as the one constant and comfort in a constantly changing universe. Joyce wrote, "a flasch and, rasch, it shall come to pasch, as hearth by hearth leaps live" (*FW* 594). In "That Nature is a Heraclitean Fire and of the comfort of the Resurrection," Hopkins had written,

> Flesh fade, and mortal trash
> Fall to the residuary worm; world's wildfire, leave but ash:
> In a flash, at a trumpet crash
> I am all at once what Christ is, since he was what I am . . .

Joyce from his own Catholic background readily translated Hopkins's easter "I am . . . Christ" into the Catholic easter eating of the paschal lamb, the pasch in which the Christian, in the Pauline insight into a most rare experience, without ceasing to be himself literally becomes another. Joyce used this Catholic notion of a kind of sharing in divine transsubstantiation in his own effort to express, in "transaccidentation," the way in which a literary artist and his reader become one in sharing the basic human experience of producing words. He here chooses to share Hopkins's expression of the everliving Christ as the center of the human universe in his own effort to express the centrality of HCE (and ALP) in the human verbal universe of *Finnegans Wake*. The bibulous overtones attending Joyce's spelling suggest an Irish mockery, but Joyce's welcoming of Hopkins's expression of flux and resurrection into his own climactic chapter seems to me a significant use of Catholic attitude reaching back to the Jesuit milieu which he had shared with Hopkins.

The "hearth by hearth" follows reasonably enough from the ash of the cosmic Heraclitean fire, but I suspect much more is involved. The image in Hopkins's work emerges from a Catholic devotion especially honored in the Catholic Ireland in which the young Joyce developed, devotion to the Sacred Heart of Jesus. Hopkins's best sermon expresses aspects of the devotion that Joyce would have often heard—not so well expressed, no doubt.[1] If Joyce had looked through Hopkins's poems—as I suppose he surely did—he would have been in a favorable position to see how the "heart" and the "hearth" joined in Hopkins's imagination, in relation to the "leaping live" of Christ from the tomb, of the German nun from the waters of the Kentish Knock, and of the more than Heraclitean sparks from the fallen and galled heart of the Christed chevalier.

There is little evidence that Joyce spent much time on Hopkins's poems— I suppose no direct evidence at all. He certainly read about "the famous Father Gerard Manley Hopkins" in *The Martyrology of Gorman*,[2] and numerous touches, some listed by Tindall, suggest that Joyce knew Hopkins's poems quite well. I once suggested that Joyce might have seen Hopkins's "No.35" in MS, so similar is the imagery of Stephen's brooding on the birds.[3] But I could find no definite suggestion that he had.

Tindall spends some effort in suggesting links between Joyce's work and that of Hopkins. "While the dapplegray dawn drags nearing nigh for to wake all droners that drowse in Dublin" (*FW* 585) may indeed, as Tindall thinks, echo Hopkins's "dapple-dawn-drawn Falcon," and the reference to the Dublin firm of Hopkins and Hopkins on *FW* 26 may include Gerard. The "falconplumes and jackboots" on the same page might derive from the "falcon" and "plume" of "The Windhover: to Christ our Lord," from "This Jack, joke, poor potsherd, patch, matchwood, immortal diamond" of "Heraclitean Fire," where the hard gemlike flame of Pater immortally reflects the grandeur of God, and from a word Joyce would likely love, "fallowbootfellow" of "Tom's Garland." Joyce and Hopkins both learned their words from Skeat, in goodly part, and both surely knew and used *On the Study of Words* by Richard Chenevix Trench, D.D.[4] Bishop Trench, a relative of the model for Haines, treats words, as people throughout the century delighted in doing, as "fossil poetry," and gives rich background for such exploitation of the history of words as that which Hopkins and Joyce delighted in. When I read "Man makes his own language, but he makes it as the bee makes its cells, as the bird its nest,"[5] it seemed to me I saw the genesis of "combs" in Hopkins's analogy between the lining up of cells in the fetus and the forming of lines in a poem: "Nine months she then, nay years, nine years she long Within her wears, bears, cares and combs the same" ("To R. B."). Hopkins might have gleaned half a dozen of the "Windhover's" words from Trench. His interesting effort to take advantage of both the medieval and the modern meanings, as Joyce too loved to do, shows up, for example, in "minion," where the proud knightly meaning contrasts with the degraded modern meaning. In "sillion," the only modern meaning of the word in that form, in French, is different from the medieval meaning of a field for plowing, and can reflect something of the loss of tradition that Hopkins so often mourns, as in "Eurydice." "Dangerous" in its knightly meaning expresses the Lord's mastery, and suggests in its modern meaning the risks of ignoring or opposing him.

Joyce's enjoyment of such manipulation of words is obvious, spectacular even in such a *tour de force* as "Oxen of the Sun" where the organic development of the language becomes a metaphor for the development of the child in the womb and of the human race in its Viconian cycling. A word to illustrate Joyce's attention to exploiting varied levels within the word could be "lewd" at the end of the passage in which Stephen, setting himself up as Christ the Priest, claims to be, with his post-creation, better than the Creator, better than the Virgin who brought forth the Word: "Let the lewd with faith and fervour worship" (*U* 392). The passage in Trench probably guided him: "In like manner that 'lewd,' which meant at one time no more than 'lay,' or unlearned—the 'lewd' people, the lay people—should come to signify the sinful, the vicious, is not a little worthy of note. How forcibly we are reminded here of that saying of the Pharisees of old: 'This people which knoweth not the law is cursed'; how much of their spirit must have been at work before the word could have acquired this secondary meaning!"[6] The bishop is blaming the Church of Rome for the degradation of "lewd," which might have amused Joyce and certainly fitted the word especially to Stephen's own attempt to degrade the mass, God, and Mary—a halfhearted attempt, compared to Buck's. Or perhaps it is better to see it rather as an attempt to use the most sacred aspects of Catholicism to exalt even the feeble and lying effort of Stephen to present himself to his disciples as an artist. Like Judas, he lies, in his case about the "glistering coins" which he had received from Deasy but which he tells them he had received for his song. He tells them not to fear leaving the bread to the lewd, for the magic, consecrated mead which he gives them will as the artist's ink make profitable songs. Stephen is indeed in parlous state, desperately in need of healing and nourishing milk from the promised land.

Haines (happily modeled on a relative of Bishop Trench) enters in Gothic tonality on *U* 412, and the black panther at which he had shot during the night probably was the ghost of his father, or better, perhaps, since in dealing with language he seems to be as inferior to the old bishop as Hamlet was to his warrior father, the ghost of old Trench, his grandfather—which may be related to Buck's introduction of "Shakespeare's grandfather" (*U* 18). "For this relief much thanks" ties Haines again to Hamlet and the rocks of chapter 1, and, I believe, to the relief of the absentminded beggar derived from the Wonderworker, a balm for rectal complaints (*U* 722). In this neat web of allusions I find, weaving in Stephen's "Catamite" of *U* 204 and Buck's "breechpad" of *U* 217, with numerous other hints, facts, and unfacts, the dark revelation of the homosexual relationship between Haines and Buck. The old bishop, by the way, in his treatment of "lewd," prepares for the "Anglican Ordinal" of *FW* 185 who, if only he does not have to read the vulgar truth about the human preparations for true literature in his "own rude dunsky tunga," can blame the Latin Roman Church for the degradation of spirituality and of language, and not face up to the Pharisaical "Pink 'Un" condemning Joyce and *Ulysses* not with the red badge of shame from the Catholic Whore of Babylon but with the watered-down pink badge of the effeminate Anglicans.[7]

If Joyce did spend any time with the *Deutschland* and "The Windhover: to Christ our Lord," he was in excellent position to note the Catholic and specifically Jesuit imagery of "Our heart's charity's hearth's fire" in relation to the mastering Lord, and the seemingly dead blue-bleak embers, symbols from Christ's image of himself as "fire cast to earth" as the Jews threw embers to scatter sparks and burn the rubble, falling and splitting to send forth the gold (for majesty) and vermilion (from "the worm and no man") sparks, like Shelley's words among mankind. The "Windhover's" "Ah my dear" emerges more immediately than from Herbert from Hopkins's own emotional reaction to the piercing of the heart of Christ. Joyce could readily see all that, prepared for it in his Catholic and Jesuit milieu, and he might also see the Heraclitean fire with all its cosmic implications here perceived as divine love, from the bowels of Christ's misery, spreading throughout the cosmos, filling all time and space with the radiance of the Spirit: "and bluebleak embers, ah my dear, Fall, gall themselves, and gash gold-vermilion."

Joyce had linked Newman's *Glories of Mary* to Newman's motto, on his cardinal's coat of arms, "Cor ad cor loquitur." After the quotation from Newman (*P* 370), Stephen imagines the Virgin telling him and Emma to take hands: "It is one heart that loves another heart. Take hands together, my dear children, and you will be happy together and your hearts will love each other." The gooey prose well fits Stephen's sentimental Virgin, and the excess of drool suggests the grinning and maybe cynical voice of Joyce the mature ventriloquist. Joyce's contempt for the vulgarization and superstition involved in popular Irish devotion to the Sacred Heart surfaces briefly in "Eveline" and in "Grace," but he knew also the good things that Irish Catholics, like his mother, thought they saw in the devotion.

As for the heart leaping, Joyce uses that, as does Hopkins. For example, as Stephen knelt in the confessional, "his heart bounded in his breast" (*P* 402). There it was fear, and it suggests a basis for Joyce's possible empathy with Hopkins's heart, in stanza 2 of *Deutschland,* swooning (a fine Anglo-Saxon word which Joyce also favored) with terror. He could understand also why Hopkins's chivalric Jesuit heart, crouching in hiding in "The Windhover: to Christ our Lord," could stir in admiration of the bird's masterful reflection of the Word.

I imagine, too, that Joyce might well have noted, as he paged through Hopkins's poems, the involvement of "hearth" with "heart" in the *Deutschland.* Jesus as "heart's light" in stanza 30, Joyce, with his Jesuit background, would be inclined to see, I believe, in terms of the symbolic flames coming from the heart of Jesus, more specifically determined in stanza 34 with the flame burning in the heart of Christ associated with the Pentecostal flame that overshadowed Mary,

> Now burn, new born to the world,
> Double-natured name,
> The heaven-flung, heart-fleshed, maiden-furled
> Miracle-in-Mary-of-flame.

Then, in the listing of Pauline and chivalric nouns, the last line, as the later "Windhover" was to do, links the Sacred Heart with the chivalric Lord: "Our hearts' charity's hearth's fire, our thoughts' chivalry's throng's Lord." Here the Jesuit, knightly in the inner life of his thoughts, like St. Alphonsus—"the heroic breast not outward-steeled"—and a plodding laborer outside, like his Lord, ties "heart" and "hearth" intimately together. Joyce, also enormously sensitive to words and their minglings, would be sensitive also to the suggestion here of fire, like Heraclitean fire, leaping up in easter brightness, being "a dayspring to the dimness of us," being "a crimson-cresseted east." When Joyce comes to his own easter chapter, these influences might well be prominent among those that brought about his leaping hearths.

In regard to the artistic workings of the heart, Hopkins and Joyce are in full agreement. Hopkins conceives of his heart as, first of all, necessarily alone in its bower of bone, the bower being a hermitage where the private self does not expect to be touched. Hence his excitement, in stanza 1 of the *Deutschland,* when he finds the Finger of God, one of the names of the Holy Spirit, touching and, as happened to Moses before the burning bush (recalled in the "nor can foot feel, being shod" of "God's Grandeur"), seeming to threaten his very existence. In stanza 18, that touch is making words break from his artistic heart, all alone in its necessary exile. And while his heart forms the words, his brain wonders what is going on. His heart, which as a result of the Fall of Man does not need to be taught to tend toward evil, nevertheless, as constructors of lie detectors have long realized, utters truth as the brain may not. The heart draws upon the deepest mysteries of human existence, the brain can accept and operate only to its own rational limits. And the activity of his heart produces tears, which mix with a melting, madrigal joy in peculiar and mysterious fashion.

> Ah, touched in your bower of bone,
> Are you! turned for an exquisite smart,
> Have you! make words break from me here all alone,
> Do you!—mother of being in me, heart.
> O unteachably after evil, but uttering truth,
> Why, tears! is it? tears; such a melting, a madrigal start!

And now the music of the madrigal and the glee produces a line which, in its rhythm and flow on the eardrum forms a metaphor for the blood flowing so faithfully and necessarily through the heart, with three of its four anapestic beats on soft l's and r's, and the pause after "revel," occasioned by the word division, reflecting both the division in the heart's own four-chambered, two-sided structure and the excited pause in the mind faced with mystery: "Never-eldering revel and river of youth, What can it be, this glee? the good you have there of your own?"

In the final chapter of *Finnegans Wake,* in a context of the struggles in human society and in the human psyche between peace and war, love and hate, shelter and storm, Joyce builds his own music to an image almost identical with Hopkins's of the heart as in its very nature the speaker of mystery, the source of literature: "Why? Every talk has his stay, vidnis Shavarsanjivana, and all-a-dreams perhapsing under lucksloop at last are through. Why? It is a sot of a swigswag, systomy dystomy, which everabody you ever anywhere at all doze. Why? Such me" (*FW* 597). Joyce's rocking, dactylic music, "swigswag, systomy dystomy," significantly reverses the rising and hopeful motion of Hopkins. Joyce is, at this point, speaking of the low point of the predawn motions of the spirit, and a rise of annewing begins in the following paragraph, "Lok! A shaft of shivery in the act." But the contrast in the two expressions of the heart as revelatory seems to me characteristic of the young, enthusiastic, and humanly naïve Hopkins and of the mature, balanced, and profoundly perceptive Joyce. "Doze," according to the subconscious and subnescious laws governing, along with conventional conscious laws, the word of *Finnegans Wake,* not only expresses the conventional "does" of universal human activity but indicates that the "all-a-dreams" (from the depths of Lear's own spiritual tempests), which deal with "perhaps" rather than "so it is," come to us from outside our rational control (as our heartbeat also does) and give the best answer we can find to the first riddle of the universe, which can be put in many ways, one good one being "Who am I?" To find the answer "Such me," I must search me, and I must go deeper than the mind can of itself reach. On this point Hopkins and Joyce find a common ground, and they both turn to the human heart for their profoundest image.

They both approach that Scotistically central heart as an organ divided against itself. Stephen, reflecting a great deal of Joyce's own experience, tends to see his soul as imprisoned in his body in Platonic fashion, and his body as a temptation and a hindrance to flight, as a tomb from which his soul should soar "in an air beyond the world and the body he knew was purified in a breath and delivered of incertitude and made radiant and commingled with the element of the spirit . . . cerements shaken from the body of death" (*P* 431). Hopkins speaks of the heart drawn to evil but, naturally good, speaking the truth; he compares his soul to a skylark scanted in a dull cage; he looks upon the "flung prouder form" of a beautiful body as a temptation drawing one from spiritual beauty. How much of this enmity between soul and body the two artists felt emerged from their Catholicism I cannot determine, but some of it did. And I see them developing in reaction to this early conviction, at least in part, in similar ways. Joyce veered so far away from his early Romantic worship of the soul that he may have come rather close to Bloom's doctrine of the soul being only the gray matter in the skull. Hopkins suffered through the tensions at least partly brought on by his distrust of his body, until at last he found some semi-Joycean relief in facing up to his own bathroom noises.

In calling himself "this Jack, joke" and "Man Jack the man is," Hopkins seems to me entering into the jackass situation of Bottom, and, in so doing, emphasizing rather than denying his use of St. Paul. The long tradition of smart asses of which Shakespeare makes generous use in such uneducated and muddleheaded clowns as Bottom and Dogberry ("O, that I had been writ down an ass!" [*Much Ado* 4. 2. 90]), who pierce through to the true undeterred by the rational evasions of their "betters," has been written about exhaustively. Less noted, to my knowledge, is Shakespeare's subtle use of St. Paul, even in so obvious a parallel as that Bottom presents, and not at all, in so far as I have been able to discover, in a more delicate reference. *The Merchant of Venice* leaves open the question as to whether the Christians of the city are not in reality more depraved than the Jews they condemn and exploit (like the Dubliners of *Ulysses*). I find some evidence in a Pauline reference, which itself is related to Bottom's "I have had a most rare vision." In 2 Cor. 12: 1, Paul speaks of the rarest of his visions: "It is not expedient for me to rejoyce:

for I wil come to visions and revelation of the Lord." The passage which Shakespeare had in mind for his thoroughly depraved Christian clown, named with bitter irony Launcelot, is the following from 2 Cor. 11—

> Of the Jewes five times received I fortie stripes save one, I was thrise beaten with roddes: I was once stoned: I suffered thrise shipwracke: night and day have I bene in ye depe sea. In jornaying I was often, in perils of waters, in perils of robbers, in perils of mine owne nation, in perils among the Gentiles, in perils in the citie, in perils in wildernes, in perils in ye sea, in perils amongst false brethren. . . . But at a windowe was I let downe in a basket through the wall, and escaped his hands.

Launcelot Gobbo, who calls his master the Jew a devil, engages like Zoe and Molly and the enchantress of the Villanelle in some commerce with the devil by fortunetelling, and in the course of so doing paraphrases, like Bottom, St. Paul, suggesting however commerce with "The Sisters Three" like Macbeth's witches, rather than like honest Bottom rejoicing in the hazy dream of the love of a good spirit.

> Well, if any man in Italy have a fairer table which doth offer to swear upon a book, I shall have good fortune. Go to, here's a simple line of life. Here's a small trifle of wives—alas, fifteen wives is nothing! A 'leven widows and nine maids is a simple coming-in for one man. And then to 'scape drowning thrice, and to be in peril of my life with the edge of a feather bed—here are simple scapes. Well, if Fortune be a woman, she's a good wench for this gear. Father, come. I'll take my leave of the Jew in the twinkling of an eye. (2. 2. 166–77)

A Catholic eye, at least one lacking any dogma of Shakespearean anti-Semitism, has little trouble in seeing here the possibility of a contrast between the loving journey in the service of a Jew and providential escape of Paul, and the viciously selfish lustful plots and scapes of this traitor to another Jew. And some of such Catholic vision in James Augusta (cf. *Ellmann*, p. 20: "The second child, James Augusta [as the birth was incorrectly registered]") Aloysius Joyce, as I conceive the matter, helped to bring about the existence of the Jew Leopold Paula Bloom, around whose personality Catholic Dublin comes to judgment in amazing and mysterious ways.

I suspect that at least two causalities brought about Bloom's middle name. He is the new apostle to the Gentiles, and he does operate, as I see him, in a Bottom context which involves the vision of St. Paul. He reflects the personality of his creator, and thus, since Joyce's official middle name is a feminine form of the name of the great Doctor to whom is fittingly attributed that "O felix culpa" which rings through *FW*, a phrase expressive of Augustine's insight drawn from Paul, especially from Rom. 5:17, it is most fitting that Bloom's name reflect a similar situation. Issy's saucy footnote on *FW* 307, "and as for that hippofoxphiz, unlucky number, late for the christening!" reflects the connection Joyce perceived between Augustine and Paul: the bishop of Hippo, foxy in his dealings with the Orthodox churches and trickily late for his own christening, heard the marvelous song (*Confessions,* 8, chap. 13) which brought about that conversion, when the innocent voice told him to take up the book and read, and found the unlucky number a source of life as he turned to Paul's words in Rom. 13:13: "Sicut in die honeste ambulemus, non in comessationibus et ebrietatibus, non in cubilibus et impudicitiis, non in contentione et aemulatione." It is a feminine, peace-loving impulse (an Orthodox churchman might mutter "O ferax cupla!" [*FW* 606]) that flowed from Paul to Augustine, in a way also from Joyce to Bloom, and in clearer ways from ALP through Mercius and Justius in the end of chapter 7 and through chapter 8 and through HCE and the whole of humanity in this great book's final lucky pages.

I suppose that one reason distinguishing Hopkins's use of St. Paul from that of Shakespeare and of Joyce is that Hopkins found himself more personally committed and more formally restrained in his manipulation of Paul's text. But I do believe that, as Hopkins developed out of his early narrow enthusiasms, as intense as Stephen's, he found, as Augustine and Shakespeare and Joyce did, that Paul had reaches that no extremes of human experience could exhaust. Thus in the great resurrection sonnet to which Joyce found himself able to respond and of which he makes apt use, the common depths are in part those of the Catholic and the Jewish traditions operative also in Shakespeare and Augustine and Paul.

There are interesting effects in the artistic products of Joyce and of Hopkins in regard to their developing acceptance of the flesh as good. Joyce proceeded from an original romanticisation of the soul as good and the flesh as evil to an eventual celebration of the flesh as the proper object of veneration in both aspects, as in Bloom's worship of Molly and Molly's own wholehearted acceptance of her own body, and above all as in the magnificently poetic celebration of the elements of water and air so perfectly and regeneratively blended in Anna Livia. Hopkins began with a Puritanically restrained suppression of the body, as in "The Habit of Perfection," with its "Elected Silence," "lovely-dumb" lips, "Be shelled, eyes, with double dark," and, most suggestive of all, this control of the senses in favor of the soul,

> Palate, the hutch of tasty lust,
> Desire not to be rinsed with wine:
> The can must be so sweet, the crust
> So fresh that come in fasts divine!

It is a huge space from this withdrawal from the outside world to Hopkins's utter abandonment in "To R. B." to open-armed welcome of outside reality, in a vivid image combining Heraclitean fire (now in a newly invented blowtorch) with the sheer delight of sexual penetration and conception. Now it is not an idea, a spiritual intuition which penetrates his rib cage, his "bower of bone," and touches his heart with an insight into God's operation, as in the

Deutschland. It is some dynamically existing other being, a bluebell or a hawk or a musical composition of Purcell, which penetrates his spirit and sires a poem in his imagination—precisely the image that Stephen developed in his gooey religious context of the seraph coming to the Virgin's chamber to announce the Word's taking on flesh. In perhaps the most beautiful poem he produced, Hopkins finds, at long last, the religious good which expresses itself in human flesh and in humanity's reflection of the generation of the Word and of Love inside the Trinity.

> The fine delight that fathers thought; the strong
> Spur, live and lancing like the blowpipe flame,
> Breathes once and, quenched faster than it came,
> Leaves yet the mind a mother of immortal song.
>
> ("To R. B.")

But he evidences now no distrust of the body, and no Platonic notion of the soul imprisoned in the body, "a skylark scanted in a dull cage" which must await the resurrection for its true freedom. There will be of course, as "Heraclitean Fire" so magnificently, and with none of the dogmatic limitation which mars such a promising effort as "To What Serves Mortal Beauty," asserts, an extraordinary new power in the risen body, as Hopkins can imagine it. In these later poems, as in the muscular and beautiful music of "Harry Ploughman," Hopkins no longer displays the determined celibate's blinking at the attractiveness of the "flung prouder form than Purcell tune lets tread to." The Catholic dogma of the Incarnation most deeply implies that both words and flesh can be divinized and more beautiful than reason, or anything else merely human, can comprehend, and both Hopkins and Joyce developed that implication to almost divine artistic achievement.

Both of them were deeply concerned with what happens to the human "I," also of concern to theology and philosophy. Both understood, perhaps in varying degrees, the implications of God's name, "I am," where the pronoun and the verb refer to the identical infinite act of existence, and the created person's "I am," where the self signified by the pronoun is distinct from the finite act of existence. Bloom writes the divine name, and then adds "a," the indefinite article which necessarily introduces an abstraction. The difficulties or painful limitations involved in producing some noun, also limited and inadequate, may be his reason for wiping out his writing in the sand which if completed, like that of Christ facing the would-be stoners of the woman taken in adultery, might have shamed the Molly-haters into departing one by one.

Stephen in "Scylla and Charybdis" had brooded over his personal identity, his self or "I," with background of Locke's somewhat silly effort to constitute selfhood on the basis of memory—"But I, entelechy, form of forms, am I by memory because under everchanging forms" (*U* 189)—set against the Aristotelean and Thomistic dealing with the soul, capable of becoming, in knowledge, all forms, as the enduring basis of the "I." I take it that Stephen expresses the two possibilities in punctuation, with the "I.I" expressing something like Hume's constant flux of impressions making the "I" as a constant merely a fiction, so that any given "I" in time and space is totally distinct from any other "I," and thus Stephen would not owe AE the pound, since a different "I" borrowed it. The "I,I" expresses the constant person under the flux, expressed in a vowel which lasts, and in conjunction with other lasting vowels expresses fully Stephen's debt, "A.E.I.O.U." All these concerns with "I" flow into Stephen's eucharistic image later in "Oxen," where the ink that makes those vowels lasting on sheepskin (or as with Shem on human skin) identifies with the mead (or wine) in which the artist's "I," like that of Christ under the appearance of wine, will share his life with those who willingly imbibe.

Hopkins expresses this same Catholic theological interest perhaps most clearly in the conclusion of "Heraclitean Fire," where he conceives of man's "common nature" as "Jack," of the "mortal trash" or ephemeral physical components of man as various incomplete or cheap materials, and of the ultimate self as "immortal diamond," which, when it is filled with and reflecting the beauty of God's infinite light, will transform all that is mortal into itself.

> Across my foundering deck shone
> A beacon, an eternal beam. Flesh fade, and mortal trash
> Fall to the residuary worm; world's wildfire, leave but ash:
> In a flash, at a trumpet crash,
> I am all at once what Christ is, since he was what I am, and
> This Jack, joke, poor potsherd, patch, matchwood, immortal diamond,
>
> Is immortal diamond.

The "Is" in that final brief line expresses not only the mortal "is" of the human "I" but the infinite "IS" which is the name of God, the "El" or the Tetragammaton as both Hopkins and Joyce are accustomed to it in Catholic tradition.

Hopkins constantly, in almost every poem he allowed to survive, stresses this principal Pauline point inherent in the doctrine of the Mystical Body, the sharing of the divine "is," the mystical identity between the Infinite Word and the Christian. Joyce uses the same doctrine to elevate in his imagery the human word which is the flesh to which he wishes to cling, with which he desires to become one flesh: "My unchanging Word is sacred. The word is my Wife, to expose and expound, to vend and to velnerate, and may the curlews crown our nuptias! Till Breath us depart! Wamen" (*FW* 167). Hopkins's union with the Word and his earlier treatment of the "I" being divinized and raised to a mysterious and rationally incomprehensible state of being is expressed in his striking Scotistic celebration of the self of all created things. Only the spiritual self, that being which is "form of forms," and can reflect on its own self in operation, can be called a person or an "I" for Hopkins, and it is this contrast that Hopkins sets up here, as in "The Windhover: to Christ our Lord" he sets up the same contrast between himself as a spiritual creature and the bird as a nonspiritual one—the basis for his admiration not of "the bird" but of "a bird." Not the individual but the kind of thing this individual embodies calls for his wonder and admiration— something like the situation in the final words of *Finnegans Wake,* where five indefinite articles give way to one definite article, which must introduce not an abstraction but an existing and therefore necessarily mysterious being. In the following poem, Hopkins states that birds, flies, stones, harps, bells, all speak the self that is in them, and to stress that all mortal things are made to do that, turns with several purposes in mind to the words of Christ before Pilate: "Pilate said to him, 'So you are a king?' Jesus answered 'You say that I am a king. For this was I born, and for this I have come into the world, to bear witness to the truth' " (*John* 18:37).

These words, to a mind which has developed in Catholic tradition, operate in the context of Christ's divinity, so that in his very being he is truth. Thus his "I" is a synonym for the fullness of scriptural justice and for divine life, which is "grace." In the octet of his sonnet, the "I" in line 8, while paraphrased from Christ's own statement, is considered as being proper to any created, mortal being, since each one, if it could verbalize its own activity, could and would say, "What I do is me"—I am made for an end, I have a proper activity fitted to my nature. But there is a mysterious and wonderful shift in the "I" which begins the sestet, the mystery stressed more by Paul than by anyone else—the identity between Christian and Christ, the fact that, "I am what he is, since he was what I am." This "I" is indeed Hopkins, but Hopkins like the "me" of the first line of the *Deutschland,* a representative Christian, illustrating the mystic truth of Paul's cry in Gal. 2: "I live now, not I, but Christ lives in me." His "I" says more than the "I" of a bird or even of a human can say. His "I" now says not only his own human personality but the divine personality of Christ, that same "everliving life" which Stephen uses as the basis of his image for the art product as eucharist: "a priest of eternal imagination, transmuting the daily bread of experience into the radiant body of everliving life" (*P* 490)—

> As kingfishers catch fire, dragonflies draw flame;
>   As tumbled over rim in roundy wells
>   Stones ring; like each tucked string tells, each hung bell's
> Bow swung finds tongue to fling out broad its name;
> Each mortal thing does one thing and the same:
>   Deals out that being indoors each one dwells;
>   Selves—goes itself; *myself* it speaks and spells,
> Crying *What I do is me: for that I came.*

> I say more: the just man justices;
>   Keeps grace: that keeps all his going graces;
>   Acts in God's eye what in God's eye he is—
> Christ. For Christ plays in ten thousand places,
> Lovely in limbs, and lovely in eyes not his
>   To the Father through the features of men's faces.

Hopkins's remarkable punning on "I" and "eyes" to express the commingling of divine and human persons in one perfect operation of love foreshadows some of Joyce's techniques. Joyce knows how to shift and to employ this tonality of the longing of finite being for the infinite in his treatment of Stephen's longing for union with his own perfect word, of the Son for the Father in the Trinitarian aspects of the "Scylla and Charybdis" discussion, in the relationships among Stephen and Bloom and Molly, and supremely, as I respond to it, in the music of Anna Livia's final flowing out into the ocean of Being: "I am passing out. O bitter ending! I'll slip away before they're up. They'll never see. Nor know. Nor miss me. And it's old and old and it's sad and old it's sad and weary I go back to you, my cold father, my cold mad father, my cold mad feary father, till the near sight of the mere size of him, the moyles and moyles of it, moananoaning, makes me seasilt saltsick and I rush, my only, into your arms" (*FW* 627–28).

Both men wrote from the bowels of their misery, from the loneliness that Catholicism traces to that unhappy fall in the park. The fact that Joyce could laugh about it more than Hopkins could might be a product of national genes more than of spiritual attitudes or of relation to Catholicism, though I do judge that both men, to some extent, abused their religion. Both tried to wrest it to their own ends. Joyce depicts his own efforts, to some degree, in the phony and superstitious plots of Stephen to get God into his debt by numbering his devotions and pretending submission to the power of the Church. Hopkins in No. 69, "My own heart," records his own efforts to force God's smile upon him. Hopkins, indeed, like young Stephen, seems to have been to some extent a victim of that Manichaeism or perhaps Jansenism which the perceptive Father Devlin, editor of *The Sermons and Devotional Writings* of Hopkins, sees creeping into nineteenth-century Catholic spirituality. The struggle that both Hopkins and Stephen record, in their different ways, is expressed in this observation of Devlin: "Yet every now and again, both in his sermons and spiritual writings, there are signs of a dark opposing presupposition which he seems unable to exorcize wholly: the presupposition of the lonely will struggling grimly against *all* that is most attractive to his higher nature."[8] Stephen's will struggled against all that threatened to limit or direct any of his nature, higher or lower, in order to be free to express without any alien pressure the direct truth of his own human experience. Hopkins perversely struggled at times to avoid expressing what he felt himself to be experiencing, perhaps because, like Joyce finding his creative music so enthralling, he feared it would somehow draw him from God to something created.

They both suffered, at any rate, and both struggled, and both worked out
that lonely suffering in terms of comparisons with the devil. Both build on the
Catholic notion of hell as the deliberate choice of cosmic loneliness and exile.
Stephen adopts the stance of Milton's Satan, and Hopkins feels himself
smothered in the monstrous "fell of dark," cursed like the lost to be his
sweating self. Shem can be, at least in large part, a *commedia dell'arte* comic
devil, which Hopkins could never produce; but Hopkins does undertake a
comparison of himself with Milton's Satan, more profound and, in an
important way, more false and dangerous than Stephen's. In the very deepest
of the desolation sonnets, No. 65, Hopkins refers to an insight into Satan's
position, as seen by Catholic theology (and by Joyce), to which Milton gave
powerful expression. In *Paradise Lost,* Satan, before he begins his attack on
man, considers his own state—

> horror and doubt distract
> His troubl'd thoughts, and from the bottom stirr
> The Hell within him, for within him Hell
> He brings, and round about him, nor from Hell
> One step no more then from himself can fly
> By change of place: Now conscience wakes despair
> That slumberd, wakes the bitter memorie
> Of what he was, what is, and what must be
> Worse; of worse deeds worse sufferings must ensue.

> (4. 18 ff.)

Worse follows worse, without end, as Milton yet more clearly and powerfully
puts it, in more rational and restrained and more pointed expression, in
Paradise Regained—

> To whom the Tempter inly rackt reply'd.
> Let that come when it comes; all hope is lost
> Of my reception into grace; what worse?
> For where no hope is left, is left no fear;
> If there be worse, the expectation more
> Of worse torments me then the feeling can.
> I would be at the worst; worst is my Port,
> My harbour and my ultimate repose,
> The end I would attain, my final good.

> (3. 203 ff.)

Hopkins longs for that same end—

> No worst, there is none. Pitched past pitch of grief,
> More pangs will, schooled at forepangs, wilder wring.
> . . . .
> Here! creep,
> Wretch, under a comfort serves in a whirlwind: all
> Life death does end and each day dies with sleep.

This is along the line of "everabody you ever anywhere at all doze," but a long way down the line. In No. 69, Hopkins, addressing that soul and tormented mind and heart upon which he knows that he himself ("selfwrung, selfstrung" of No. 61) is inflicting needless suffering, gives himself friendly advice: "Soul, self; come, poor Jackself, I do advise/You, jaded, let be; call off thoughts awhile/Elsewhere; leave comfort root-room." Himself as jaded ass, the Jack and joke, approaches a Joycean treatment, and he carries the treatment as far as he can, far too much for his conventional friend and meddling editor, Bridges (possibly, as Tindall suggests, the "old Pantifox" of *FW* 293), in the second-last poem he wrote two months before he died, No. 75.

> The shepherd's brow, fronting forked lightning, owns
> The horror and the havoc and the glory
> Of it. Angels fall, they are towers, from heaven—
>   a story
> Of just, majestical, and giant groans.
> But man—we, scaffold of score brittle bones;
> Who breathe, from groundlong babyhood to hoary
> Age gasp; whose breath is our *memento mori*—
> What bass is *our* viol for tragic tones?
> He! Hand to mouth he lives, and voids with shame;
> And, blazoned in however bold the name,
> Man Jack the man is, just; his mate a hussy.
> And I that die these deaths, that feed this flame,
> That . . . in smooth spoons spy life's masque
>   mirrored: tame
> My tempests there, my fire and fever fussy.

The Heraclitean fire has merged with the "life's fitful fever" of the murderous and disillusioned Macbeth, dwindled to a drudging Greek teacher's pedantic fussiness, like that of his brother Jesuit, the dean of studies in *Portrait*. "Tame," as the several early drafts in the Bodleian notebook make clear, is an adjective, and indicates that the tempests in Lear's mind or the tempests that artistic magicians like Prospero might raise are tame in the smooth spoons which serve to bring the animal food to his unspeaking mouth, and serve also as the mirrors in which he can spy in distortion the artificial masque of his conventional life. But most Joycean touch of all, most unexpected in the prudish Romanticist who, in the *Deutschland,* paid little direct attention to the body, he measures out death with his breath, and with the gasses emerging from the other end of his digestive tract, sounds out a smelly bass most inappropriate to Miltonic tragedy. It foreshadows the conclusion of "Sirens" in *Ulysses*.

As I believe Paul Mariani was the first to note, Hopkins most probably derives his spoon image from a woman he disliked but nevertheless read. In the opening quatrain of the sonnet, Hopkins is thinking of himself in relation to Milton, the poet of *Lycidas* and of *Paradise Lost,* the greatest of elegies celebrating the drowning (like the drowning of the nun in Hopkins's elegiac ode) of a promising young poet and the greatest of epics celebrating the fall of angels (as Hopkins attempted to express the fall of Caradoc). Milton filled the world with Pentecostal winds and flames, and Hopkins thinking of his own mostly abortive efforts along the same lines, recalled, I have no doubt whatever, the vivid treatment of Milton in *Middlemarch*: "I am not sure that the greatest man of his age, if ever that solitary superlative existed, could escape these unfavorable reflections of himself in various small mirrors; and even Milton, looking for his portrait in a spoon, must submit to have the facial angle of a bumpkin."[9] The discussion of Eliot's commentator in the rest of the paragraph—"what fading of hopes, or what deeper fixity of self-delusion" and "Mr. Casaubon, too, was the center of his own world; if he was liable to think that others were providentially made for him . . . this trait is not quite alien to us"—also follows the bitter line of Hopkins, who, like Bloom, sees himself and his small world distorted in a mirror, which for Hopkins also reminds him, to his disgust, that he too (like Molly Bloom and Poldy) is a gaseous beast.

But that disgust seems to me a most healthy thing in Hopkins, and a symptom of greater spiritual health. I should think that if he can accept his animality, if he can get rid of the tendency (also apparent in the phony piety of the "converted" Stephen of the opening of *Portrait*'s chapter 4) to ignore and suppress his body, he might relax a bit and enjoy life more, and he might avoid artistic perversities like the final line of No. 62, where "God's better beauty, grace" seems to be dragged in to tone down the beauty of those wet-fresh lads, so admired by old Gregory. Not that Hopkins was always crippled by scrupulous fears of the too-attractive created things around him—witness the magnificent No. 71, with its sinewy music creating in language the strength and grace of Harry Ploughman in a way that Joyce, perhaps with a cynical smile, would admire. Hopkins's willingness to see in "The shepherd's brow" the self, destined for union with Christ, actually existing and operating on a jackass level is in a way solid earthy basis and preparation for the construction of his last and possibly most beautiful poem. In "To R. B.," Hopkins compares himself as artist, as Joyce does in comparing himself to the Blessed Virgin bringing forth the Word, to a mother conceiving and gestating a baby. The conception results from the happily delightful coition between his own mind and another real being (like Stephen with the Ballast Office clock, *SH* 211) and in this perfect poem Hopkins, in Wildean paradox, mourns his inability to produce one.

To R. B.
The fine delight that fathers thought; the strong
Spur, live and lancing like the blowpipe flame,
Breathes once and, quenchèd faster than it came,
Leaves yet the mind a mother of immortal song.

Nine months she then, nay years, nine years she long
Within her wears, bears, cares and combs the same:
The widow of an insight lost she lives, with aim
Now known and hand at work now never wrong.

Sweet fire the sire of muse, my soul needs this;
I want the one rapture of an inspiration.
O then if in my lagging lines you miss
The roll, the rise, the carol, the creation,
My winter world, that scarcely breathes that bliss
Now, yields you, with some sighs, our explanation.

Hopkins's treatment of the beastly situation of "Man Jack" is not less Catholic than is his Pauline treatment of man as identified with Christ, "Acts in God's eye what in God's eye he is—Christ" (No. 57). It is a completion of his Catholic vision, not a denial of it. It is an acceptance, like simple and honest Bottom's, of his asininity as well as of the Fairy Queen's embrace. It increases the wonder, and the beauty. It is this aspect of Joyce's work that I believe needs stressing too, that his celebration of the beastly aspects of man's situation, while it may be an overreaction to the kind of suppression he found in Catholic Ireland, which was eager to perceive water made into wine but reluctant to admit that the wine again made water, does nevertheless serve rather to elevate the human than to drag down the divine. Like Clive Hart, I find beauty in Molly's chamber pot, musically filled with her blood and urine, serving as an image for the consecrated chalice, filled with the blood and water which poured, as in the final image of "The Windhover: to Christ our Lord," from the side of Christ to offer divinity to asinine humans. It strikes me that no harm need thereby come to the chalice, but that the human good there is in the pot is at least artistically enhanced as much as human skill can achieve. I rejoice to see Hopkins become more Joycean, and I see Joyce coming closer, in his maturity, to Hopkins's Jesuit appreciation of things Catholic and divine. They both can in somewhat different senses be called Catholic artists, as I see them, as I suppose, they both can be called Greek artists. The *Britannica* article oversimplifies, I judge, when it calls Joyce "fiercely anti-Catholic."

The point is a cloudy one, but important. As I can grasp it, the literary artist succeeds when he expresses effectively his human experience. The experience of a man who says "yes" to divine faith will be quite different, I should judge, from that of the man who says "no." Yet they are basically alike in that both are human, and both deal necessarily with the human mystery that lies beyond reason. If they will like Bottom (and Hippolyta) accept and admire the strange, their human reactions to it, while different, are equally valid and interesting and valuable for literature. The aim is not to advance the abstract truth nor to improve society nor to give glory to God. The aim is

solely to contemplate, with the dynamic stasis that Stephen perhaps too
rationally expressed as "the enchantment of the heart." Stephen erred in
dealing with "quidditas" instead of "ens," with an abstract and rational grasp
instead of a dynamic and intuitive apprehension. Hopkins in "To R. B."
knows that it is the ephemeral grasp of being which inseminates the mind and
heart so that a poem expressive of total human experience can take form. The
mature Joyce knows (or apprehends) that too and expresses it best of all in
such passages as that on *FW* 118. There he faces the seeming contradiction
between the fact that "every person, place and thing in the chaosmos of Alle
anyway connected with the gobblydumped turkery was moving and changing
every part of the time," and the effort of the artist to get this Heraclitean flux
expressed in the seemingly static but, through the magic and music of the
artist, "changeably meaning vocable scriptsigns." The principle behind
Joyce's dealing with language in *FW,* or one of the principles, can be
discerned in the hidden meaning of this writing on the wall, which expresses
not only the rational cosmos but the chaos which flows without pause through
all. Theseus with rational complacency wants clarity, aims to reduce the
words and acts and motives of others to rational comprehension (he condemns
imaginative apprehension), and rejects the strange in favor of the abstract
truth. Joyce in his passage speaks first, I believe, in the spirit of Shem, and
ironically toward the end moves into the voice of Shaun, actually quoting
Wyndham Lewis's Theseus-like condemnation of *Work in Progress* with the
supercilious "This will never do." First Theseus—

> More strange than true. I never may believe
> These antique fables, nor these fairy toys.
> Lovers and madmen have such seething brains,
> Such shaping fantasies, that apprehend
> More than cool reason ever comprehends.
> The lunatic, the lover, and the poet
> Are of imagination all compact.
> One sees more devils than vast Hell can hold,
> That is the madman. The lover, all as frantic,
> Sees Helen's beauty in a brow of Egypt.
> The poet's eye, in a fine frenzy rolling,
> Doth glance from heaven to earth, from earth to heaven,
> And as imagination bodies forth
> The forms of things unknown, the poet's pen
> Turns them to shapes, and gives to airy nothing
> A local habitation and a name.
> Such tricks hath strong imagination
> That if it would but apprehend some joy,
> It comprehends some bringer of that joy;
> Or in the night, imagining some fear,
> How easy is a bush supposed a bear!

(MND 5. 1. 2 ff.)

And now Joyce, giving shifting habitations and protean names to the forms of things beyond the comprehensions of any of us:

Because, Soferim Bebel, if it goes to that, (and dormerwindow gossip will cry it from the housetops no surelier than the writing on the wall will hue it to the mod of men that mote in the main street) every person, place and thing in the chaosmos of Alle anyway connected with the gobblydumped turkery was moving and changing every part of the time: the travelling inkhorn (possibly pot), the hare and turtle pen and paper, the continually more and less intermisunderstanding minds of the anticollaborators, the as time went on as it will variously inflected, differently pronounced, otherwise spelled, changeably meaning vocable scriptsigns. No, so holp me Petault, it is not a miseffectual whyacinthinous riot of blots and blurs and bars and balls and hoops and wriggles and juxtaposed jottings linked by spurts of speed: it only looks as like it as damn it; and, sure, we ought really to rest thankful that at this deleteful hour of dungflies dawning we have even a written on with dried ink scrap of paper at all to show for ourselves, tare it or leaf it, (and we are lufted to ourselves as the soulfisher when he led the cat out of the bout) after all that we lost and plundered of it even to the hidmost coignings of the earth and all it has gone through and by all means, after a good ground kiss to Terracussa and for wars luck our lefftoff's flung over our home homoplate, cling to it as with drowning hands, hoping against hope all the while that, by the light of philophosy, (and may she never folsage us!) things will begin to clear up a bit one way or another within the next quarrel of an hour and be hanged to them as ten to one they will too, please the pigs, as they ought to categorically, as, stricly between ourselves, there is a limit to all things so this will never do. (FW 118-19)

Theseus and Joyce take different views of reality, of the imagination, and of literature. Shakespeare, I take it, stands with Bottom and with Joyce in accepting the chaos of the cosmos and yet in supposing that the artist's miracle will have might enough to express the inexpressible in black ink. Hopkins too judges that by some mysterious inspiration he can as artist express the roll, the rise, the carol, the creation. Music will do it where sheer reason must fail. Puck at the end of *MND* speaks to the Theseuses in the Globe audience who may have been offended, as Lewis was by *FW,* and, a mere shadow himself, tells them to be kindly in their solid materiality.

> If we shadows have offended,
> Think but this, and all is mended,
> That you have but slumbered here
> While these visions did appear,
> And this weak and idle theme,
> No more yielding but a dream.

It is the dream that St. Paul tells all men that their eyes and ears will never achieve, the dream that Hopkins paradoxically expressed in his winter-world mourning that he cannot express, the dream that Joyce expresses in magic pages that surpass in beauty and mystery for me even the most beautiful music of *The Tempest,* those final pages of *FW* where the water and the woman carry us into humanity as Hopkins carries us into God, "Stanching, quenching ocean of a motionable mind," and we understand, maybe, that the depths of human reality are not to be found in the streets of London outside the Globe, but in the shadows inside us that really are more strange than true, that drop us into mystery with sounds.

We pass through grass behush the bush to. Whish!

Notes   Index

Notes

Foreword: "Man is but an Asse"

1. In a book so well known among late-Victorian students of words that it is morally certain that both Hopkins and Joyce knew and used it, *On the Study of Words* by Richard Chenevix Trench, D.D., (London: George Routledge and Sons Ltd. [1851]), the following passage dealing with a commonplace distinction and involving an analogy between religion and literature might have been of interest to both—

> As involving in like manner a distinction which cannot safely be lost sight of, how important the difference, of which the existence is asserted by our possession of the two words, "to apprehend" and "to comprehend," with their substantives, "apprehension," and "comprehension." For indeed we "apprehend" many truths, which we do not "comprehend." The great mysteries of our faith,—the doctrine for instance of the Holy Trinity, we lay hold upon it (ad prehendo), we hang on it, our souls live by it; but we do not "*com*prehend" it, that is, we do not take it all in; for it is a necessary attribute of God that He is *incomprehensible;* if He were not so, either He would not be God, or the being that comprehended Him would be God also. . . . But I read *Hamlet*, or *King Lear*: here I "apprehend" much; I have wondrous glimpses of the poet's intention and aim; but I do not for an instant suppose that I have "comprehended," taken in, that is, all that was in his mind in the writing. (Pp. 202–3)

Shakespeare's own attention to those terms appears in Theseus' speech at the opening of act 5 of *MND*.

2. "So that Glugg, the poor one, in that limbopool which was his subnesciousness he could scares of all knotknow" (*FW* 224). This word, deeper than subconsciousness, refers, as I can read it, both to incomprehensible musical intuitions ("And bids him tend her, lute and airly. Sing, sweetharp, thing to me anone!"), which Glugg experiences as he gestates beneath the human heartbeat in the womb, and to his (and

every human person's) intuitive apprehension of the mysteries of reality. It helps to stress one of the principles of Joyce's treatment of language in *FW*, explicated further in such passages as: "Helldsdend, whelldselse! Lonedom's breach lay foulend up uncouth not be broched by punns and reedles" (*FW* 239). The "belchybubhub" in the previous line expresses the "subnesciousness," which puns and riddles cannot quite reach, to breach the unknowing mind's uncouth foul end so that it might wet the tea, fecundate the godlike potency for producing magic and divine ink.

3. "One of the objects literally present is undoubtedly the 'ass them four old codgers owns' (214.33), but a close inspection of the passage before us leaves me uncertain whether this can be taken as anything but metaphor here. The donkey may be supposed to be telling this part of the story, but a few pages later we find Shaun himself seemingly addressed as the donkey: 'salve a tour, ambly andy' (409.31). This is complicated by 'salve a tour' which seems to say *Salvator*. It has been said that Joyce is describing the donkey as Christ, but it seems more likely that this is Shaun who is, one must remember, performing a *via crucis*." *A Conceptual Guide to Finnegans Wake,* ed. Michael H. Begnal and Fritz Senn (University Park: Pennsylvania State University Press, 1974), pp. 153-54. Hereafter *Conceptual Guide*.

4. "It seems likely that the passing reference to *Huckleberry Finn*: 'those pedestriasts Top, Sind and Hucky' refers to the chapters at Aunt Sally's when Tom was Sid and Huck was Tom. Identities are constantly changing so that it is no wonder that Shaun has difficulty trying 'to isolate i from my multiple Mes' (510.12)." *Conceptual Guide,* p. 154 (The reference should be to 410.12.)

1. Mad Winthrop's Delugium Stramens

1. William Butler Yeats, *Mythologies* (New York: Collier Books, 1969), p. 275.

2. The Latin paraphrase of Psalm 81:3 on *FW* 412, lines 8-9, could be translated, "Blow in Emenia the horn worthy of your voluminousness," and refers, as "mielodorous" (suggestive of *mel* or honey and the fragrance of the Song of Song's bridegroom) and "after draught" hint, to the kind of music with which Bloom ends the "Sirens" chapter in *Ulysses*.

3. Cf. The extremely valuable article "The Fourfold Moses in *Ulysses*," by Roderick Davis, *James Joyce Quarterly* 7, no. 2 (Winter 1970): 120-31.

2. To Tara via Holyhead

1. *Herring* refers to *Joyce's Ulysses Notesheets in the British Museum*, ed. Phillip F. Herring (Charlottesville: University Press of Virginia, 1972).

2. " 'Ithaca's' Westward-turning Earth: A New Portal of Discovery in *Ulysses*," *James Joyce Quarterly* 7, no. 4 (Summer 1970): 371-73.

3. In *James Joyce's Dubliners, Critical Essays,* ed. Clive Hart (London: Faber and Faber, 1969), 153-69.

4. *The Ordeal of Stephen Dedalus* (Carbondale: Southern Illinois University Press, 1971): "Stephen, therefore, leaves the house of bondage and goes on his way under the chariot of David. As he goes, a Jew's harp sounds in Eccles Street for the beginning of his life as the new David, the mature creator, and the dawn prepares to rise" (p. 173).

5. Cf. Clive Hart, *Structure and Motif in Finnegans Wake* (Evanston, Ill.: Northwestern University Press, 1962), p. 207.

6. E. L. Epstein, in a stimulating discussion in "Chance, Doubt, Coincidence, and the Prankquean's Riddle," *A Wake Newslitter* 6, no. 1 (February 1969), also finds the Trinity involved in the Riddle, so that one gloss of the question might be "Why do the

members of the Trinity resemble each other so completely?" In his brief discussion, he notes that Stephen (and perhaps he means to imply Joyce as well) accepts the law of chance, rather than the law of divine determination, as the source of raw material for his art. The incertitude that attracts both Stephen and Joyce does not exclude divine determination but simply makes the purely rational assertion of it impossible. Joyce in building on rational incertitude, as Christ himself did, actually admits the implications of the Catholic position on the mystery of human freedom of choice in relation to the infinite freedom of God. There is no rational way to demonstrate that those can coexist, yet there is no absolute proof that in ways inaccessible to human reason they are also and necessarily irreconcilable. Catholic faith accepts what it asserts to be the witness of God that both human freedom and divine determination exist and operate, and that it exceeds the limits of human reason to comprehend how. Joyce (though possibly not the young Stephen), as I can comprehend his position, neither asserts nor rules out the Catholic position, and thus is in a splendid position to use the Church also for the raw materials of his art.

I am much drawn (though I suspect on somewhat different ultimate bases from his) to what seems to me the brilliant insight of David Daiches in "What Was the Modern Novel?" in *Critical Inquiry* 1, no. 4 (June 1975): "The humour of *Finnegans Wake* is at the opposite pole from the kind of humour which Sterne evoked from the verbal encounters between Walter and Toby Shandy. The multiple pun is the last refuge of relativism; it implies that everything might be true and, indeed, that everything can really be considered as everything else. Far from being obsessive the multiple pun is the last word in sceptical tolerance" (p. 818). As long as that skepticism does not harden into dogma, like the absolute domination of chance Epstein attributes to Stephen, I judge that Daiches's expression is exact and revealing, and the "last refuge" image an apt one for Joyce's treatment of language in *FW,* where the artistic fox turns at bay in the very sources of human language, before rational meanings are yet fully determined, and in his sly and subtle music and puns allows a few trailing clouds of subnescious glory to survive.

Daiches's remarks on "the new concept of time and its relation to consciousness," so important to Joyce throughout his work, enforce Joyce's insight into the processional being of the word, its similarity to the "present instant" in not existing at all as an objective, independent entity. One brilliant Trinitarian expression of James's "specious present" theory can be found at the close of the Gracehoper's song of forgiveness, where "beating time" is of the essence. The Father as the "already" and the Son as the "not yet" blend in and breathe forth that self-consuming Flame (Milton in *Samson Agonistes* calls the Phoenix a holocaust) which serves here as an infinite symbol of the finite process of time and of literature, common to allflesh: "In the name of the former and of the latter and of their holocaust. Allmen" (*FW* 419). This foreshadows the agricultural treatment of the Trinity, flowing into the timely Quinet sentence, and in the context of the "wholemole millwheeling vicociclometer" of literature and specifically of *FW,* as it approaches that final "the" which will propel it back to the "exprogressive process" of "riverrun, past Eve and Adam's" or out into subnescious eternity or nonbeing: "(for the farmer, his son and their homely codes, known as eggburst, eggblend, eggburial and hatch-as-hatch can)" (*FW* 614).

I should like here also to acknowledge the usefulness of the valuable dissertation of Patrick A. McCarthy, "The Riddles of *Finnegans Wake*" (University of Wisconsin-Milwaukee, 1973). He and I had many discussions of the matters treated here, and I am especially indebted to him for his treatment of Jarl's name in relation to the Tetragrammaton.

7. In his remarkably illuminating and penetrating "The Rhythmic Gesture: Image and Aesthetic in Joyce's *Ulysses,*" ELH 29, no. 1 (March 1962), p. 88.

8. "On that mystery and not on the madonna which the cunning Italian intellect flung to the mob of Europe the church is founded" (*U* 207). The Vatican, specifically

St. Peter's Basilica, is throughout *FW* "the house that Jack built," which I take to be Joyce's joke on the money (or "jack") so assiduously collected, with so much attendant scandal, by "Jack" Tetzel, the preacher of indulgences in behalf of the basilica, a man and a cause both deeply offensive to Luther.

9. Cf. Zack Bowen, "Lizzie Twigg: Gone but not Forgotten," *James Joyce Quarterly* 6, no. 4 (Summer 1969) and her picture in the Winter 1969 issue. Zack quotes a representative sample of her verse, "Even-Song," which begins: "The daylight is dying, / The low breezes sighing, / The wee bird is flying home to its nest."

10. "Leonardo of Pisa," *James Joyce Quarterly* 7, no. 2 (Winter 1969): 148–50.

11. Only once, I believe, is the number spelled out, "with a villa and eight rooms" (*U* 758).

12. In "Molly's Masterstroke," *Ulysses: Fifty Years,* ed. Thomas F. Staley (Bloomington: Indiana University Press, 1974), pp. 19–28.

3. "A fortifine popespriestpower bull of attender to booth"

1. —What are you reading now, captain? Dixon asked. *The Bride of Lammermore?*

—I love old Scott, the flexible lips said. I think he writes something lovely. There is no writer can touch sir Walter Scott.

He moved a thin shrunken brown hand gently in the air in time to his praise and his thin quick eyelids beat often over his sad eyes.

Sadder to Stephen's ear was his speech: a genteel accent, low and moist, marred by errors: and listening to it he wondered was the story true and was the thin blood that flowed in his shrunken frame noble and come of an incestuous love? (*P* 497).

2. "When, in a Farm Street sermon, he compared the grace-dispensing visible Church to a milch cow wandering through the pastures of the world and offering its full udders (the Sacraments) to all who sought them, he was cultivating the commonplace in the manner of a seventeenth-century poet or a Welsh country minister but not in a manner which would please a conventional Victorian upper-class congregation." W. H. Gardner, *Gerard Manley Hopkins* (London: Oxford University Press, 1949), 2:46.

3. "And the damned are so utterly bound and helpless that, as a blessed saint, saint Anselm, writes in his book on similitudes, they are not even able to remove from the eye a worm that gnaws it" (*P* 374).

4. "So then they got the keys and opened the chapel and the clerk and Father O'Rourke and another priest that was there brought in a light for to look for him" (*D* 28).

5. In a particularly lovely passage of a Latin eucharistic hymn ("In Festo Nativitatis, Ad Matrem Virginem, Hymnus Eucharisticus," *The Poems of Gerard Manley Hopkins,* ed. W. H. Gardner and N. H. MacKenzie [London: Oxford University Press, 1967], pp. 220–21), Hopkins has several images not alien to Joyce's treatment of the Word made flesh, particularly this one of the Word rendered speechless. Addressing Mary, Hopkins says,

> Demum quid sensisti
> Ipsum cum vidisti
> Tandem visu pleno
> Parvulum in foeno,
> Ecce tremebundum
> Qui fixum firmat mundum
> Et involutum pannos

Qui aeternos annos
Nondum natus de te
Volvebat in quiete?
Quae tu tum dicebas
Et quae audiebas?
Etsi fuit mutus
Tamen est locutus.
Da complecti Illum,
Mihi da pauxillum
Tuo ex amore
Et oscula ab ore.
Qui pro me vult dari,
Infans mihi fari,
Mecum conversari,
Tu da contemplari,
Mater magni Dei,
Mater Jesu mei.

which can freely be translated: "Finally what did you feel when finally you saw Him in plain view, the little one in the hay. Behold all atremble the one who made firm the fixed universe, and rolled around with cloths the one who, not yet born of you, rolled around in quiet the eternal years. What were you then saying, and what were you hearing? For even though he was mute, nevertheless (being the Word himself, by existing he spoke) he was speaking. Give him to me to be embraced, and out of your love give the little one to me and the kisses of love. The One who wishes to give himself for me, unspeaking (an 'infant') to converse with me, do you give me to be contemplated, Mother of the great God, Mother of my Jesus." The "oscula ab ore" indicates how much Hopkins shared Joyce's own love of and reaction to the Song of Songs, upon which Joyce's own love songs are largely based.

6. "James Clarence Mangan," *The Critical Writings of James Joyce,* ed. Ellsworth Mason and Richard Ellmann (New York: Viking Press, 1964) p. 82.

7. *Herring* 499.

8. *Herring* 504.

9. William York Tindall, *James Joyce, His Way of Interpreting the Modern World* (New York: Charles Scribners Sons, 1950): "At this point the Jesuit fathers hold a retreat for the examination of conscience. Coldly and systematically, after the formula of Ignatius Loyola, the priest describes the odors, sights, and sounds of hell and all its pains. Stephen vomits. Horror and 'the sting of conscience' drive him to the sacrament of penance. Refusing to scratch the bites of fleas, he is ascetic and austere. If Joyce had ended hereabouts, *A Portrait of the Artist* would be the great Catholic novel; for nothing on spiritual experience in recent literature is more moving, authentic, and exemplary. But Stephen tires of pieties, and when the Jesuits, noticing his Jesuitical demeanor, ask him to become one of their number, he declines. The trouble is that the Church fails to conform to his high ideal of what a church should be. Not he but the Church is insufficiently Catholic. For Stephen's difficult case, a Jesuit advises a clerkship in Guinness' brewery" (pp. 9-10). As Joyce demonstrates that he well knew—e.g., the cash-register image after the drooling "white-rose" imagery of the penitent Stephen—to any perceptive Catholic the spiritual experience expressed here stems from the diabolical, servile fear, based in ultimate selfishness, which makes Stephen vomit.

10. "A shadow passed over his face as he remembered her sullen opposition to his marriage. Some slighting phrases she had used still rankled in his memory; she had

once spoken of Gretta as being country cute and that was not true of Gretta at all. It was Gretta who had nursed her during all her last long illness in their house at Monkstown" (*D* 203).

11. *Herring* 439.

12. "He heard then a warm heavy sigh, softer, as she turned over and the loose brass quoits of the bedstead jingled. Must get those settled really. Pity. All the way from Gibraltar. Forgotten any little Spanish she knew. Wonder what her father gave for it. Old style. Ah yes, of course. Bought it at the governer's auction. Got a short knock. Hard as nails at a bargain, old Tweedy. Yes, sir. At Plevna that was. I rose from the ranks, sir, and I'm proud of it. Still he had brains enough to make that corner in stamps. Now that was farseeing" (*U* 56).

"Now the lumpy old jingly bed always reminds me of old Cohen I suppose he scratched himself in it often enough and he thinks father bought it from Lord Napier that I used to admire when I was a little girl because I told him easy piano O I like my bed" (*U* 772).

13. The following passage gives the indirect and symbolic approach of the almost idiotically pious Stephen to his experience of an erection, showing the operation of mind characteristic of him, for example, the indirection which makes it difficult to realize, at the end of "Proteus" in *Ulysses,* that he is urinating: "The ache of conscience ceased and he walked onward swiftly through the dark streets. There were so many flagstones on the footpath of that street and so many streets in that city and so many cities in the world. Yet eternity had no end. He was in mortal sin. Even once was a mortal sin. It could happen in an instant. But how so quickly? By seeing or by thinking of seeing. The eyes see the thing, without having wished first to see. Then in an instant it happens. But does that part of the body understand or what? The serpent, the most subtle beast of the field. It must understand when it desires in one instant and then prolongs its own desire instant after instant, sinfully. It feels and understands and desires. What a horrible thing! Who made it to be like that, a bestial part of the body able to understand bestially and desire bestially? Was that then he or an inhuman thing moved by a lower soul than his soul? His soul sickened at the thought of a torpid snaky life feeding itself out of the tender marrow of his life and fattening upon the slime of lust. O why was that so? O why?" (*P* 397-98).

14.   The lunatic, the lover, and the poet
        Are of imagination all compact.

        . . . .

        The poet's eye, in a fine frenzy rolling,
        Doth glance from heaven to earth, from earth to heaven,
        And as imagination bodies forth
        The forms of things unknown, the poet's pen
        Turns them to shapes, and gives to airy nothing
        A local habitation and a name.
        Such tricks hath strong imagination
        That if it would but apprehend some joy,
        It comprehends some bringer of that joy.

                                            (*MND* 5. 1. 8 ff.)

15. Anna Livia steps in, as well as I can grasp the matter now, to tone down the "total depravity" Lutheran approach of Justius and to inject some optimistic faith into the fatalistic melancholy of Mercius—"He is cured by faith who is sick of fate" (*FW* 482)—so that on *FW* 195 she both "deloothers" and "sloothers." This seems to me connected with the "peloothered" state of Kernan, pointed out to him by Martin

Cunningham, who in the Swiftian element of "Grace," allegorizes Martin Luther (as I attempt to demonstrate in "Swiftian Allegory and Dantean Parody in Joyce's 'Grace,' " in the *James Joyce Quarterly* 7, no. 1 [Fall 1969]:11–21). Luke as tour guide on *FW* 582 strongly distinguishes Lutherans and Catholics: "(private judgers, change here for Lootherstown! Onlyromans, keep your seats!)"

4. Joyce's Esthetic

1. That the Trinitarian doctrine, the central mystery of Catholicism, was of great interest to Joyce is stressed by his special concern with the teaching on the procession of the Holy Ghost from the Father and the Son, and with the Photian schism involving the "filioque" controversy, which split East and West. *FW* 156, 8–18 deals with this Trinitarian interest, and Joyce's commentary on it, reported by Budgen, reflects the way he dwelt on the mystery in his imagination. Budgen quotes a letter (in *Letters*, 3:284) dealing with the " 'old Catholic' Augustiner Kirche" having gone from Mookse to Gripes (from Vatican doctrine to sectional variation): "But most important of all, they have abolished the *filioque* clause in the creed concerning which there has been a schism between the East and the West for over a thousand years, Rome saying that the Holy Ghost proceeded from the Father and the Son, Greece and the East Orthodox churches that the procession is from the Father alone, *ex patre* without *filioque*. Of course the dogmas subsequently proclaimed by Rome after the split are not recognized by the East, such as the Immaculate Conception—See the Mookse and the Gripes . . . that is East and West, par. beginning, 'When that Mooksus' and ending 'philioque.' All the grotesque words in this are in Russian or Greek for the three principal dogmas which separate Shem from Shaun. When he gets A and B on his lap C slips off, and when he has A and C he loses hold on B" (Frank Budgen, *James Joyce and the Making of Ulysses* [Bloomington: Indiana University Press, 1960], p. 316).

On the previous page, Budgen describes a Trinitarian image in which Joyce not only revealed some of his own broodings over the Trinitarian being of God, but indicates a most interesting similarity with one of Hopkins's equally revealing Trinitarian statements. The galley proofs of Budgen's book "were placed one after the other on Joyce's knees, from which insecure position they slithered, as is their way, a few at a time on to the floor. As soon as Joyce stooped to pick up the fallen ones others slipped off to take their place. Joyce's comment was: 'Galley proofs remind me of the persons of the Trinity. Get firm hold of one of them and you lose grip on the others' " (ibid., p. 315). The dynamism of infinite exchange of love which is at once Same and Other, the impossibility of fixing in the mind the tantalizing mystery forever beyond the reach of reason and yet essential for any satisfying resolution of human drives we all feel and intuit, the suspicion that in this central mystery lies that one Word known to all men (which Stephen demands of his mother returned from the dead)—all these, the evidence of Joyce's work indicates to me, haunted his mind as they haunted the Catholic mind and work of Hopkins. In a letter to Bridges, Hopkins used an image of the mind at work on the mystery of the Trinity which seems to me much like Joyce's "firm hold of one and you lose grip on the others": "There are three persons, each God and each the same, the one, the only God: to some people this is a 'dogma', a word they almost chew, that is an equation in theology, the dull algebra of schoolmen: to others it is news of their dearest friend or friends, leaving them all their lives balancing whether they have three heavenly friends or one—not that they have any doubt on the subject, but that their knowledge leaves their minds swinging; poised, but on the quiver. And this might be the ecstasy of interest, one would think" (*The Letters of Gerard Manley Hopkins to Robert Bridges* [London: Oxford University Press, 1955], pp. 187–88).

2. Let him oh! with his air of angels then lift me, lay me!
   only I'll
   Have an eye to the sakes of him, quaint moonmarks, to
   his pelted
      plumage under
   Wings: so some great stormfowl, whenever he has walked
   his while
   The thunder-purple seabeach plumed purple-of-thunder,
   If a wuthering of his palmy snow-pinions scatter a
   colossal smile
   Off him, but meaning motion fans fresh our wits with wonder.

3. Of all the infinitude of nouns available to Bloom when he wrote with his stick in the sand where Stephen had in the morning seen "signatures of all things I am here to read," one possibility was "boom." Bloom began (*U* 381), in his message for the woman, with the necessary starting point, "I." Then he completed the divine name "AM," but, since he is finite, he properly went on to the indefinite article which would introduce some quality or act proper to him. Owing to the happy misprint in the funeral notice, for which, as he recalls the fact that he himself distracted Nannetti's orthographical routine (cf. *U* 647 and 121–22), he may have been responsible, he does become L. Boom, which Stephen, fearer of thunder, had in a way prepared for by changing the name for God which he had given to Deasy, inspired by the relatively innocent shouts of the battling players striving for a goal, "A shout in the street" (*U* 34), to "Damn that fellow's noise in the street" (*U* 505), inspired by the grotesquely ironic blaring in Maggot Street of "The Holy City."

   I'm not sure what Stephen means by that "shout in the street," but in the context of wars, I suspect that among other things he means that God, less Deasy's sentimental construct than the Dio Boia, is the product of human breath and emotion. In "Circe," he is now speaking as a literary artist rather than as a sociologist and historian. Thus he now uses the musical octave as a symbol of the limits of man's rational constructing capacity, which can move only from the tonic up to the dominant, then start down to the tonic again, and so on around and around. The noisy, jangling, discordant interference from the loud gramophone, now not a "shout" but a "noise," disrupts his image, and illustrates that forces from outside his construct, not under his control, disprove the very point he is trying to make. "L. Boom" illustrates that the operation of unforseen chance in the production of a typographical error can enter into and influence human thought and activity. His later perception of the unexpected love in Bloom himself will deal perhaps the final and decisive blow to Stephen's not very wholehearted effort at neat Maeterlinckian rationalism (in his treatment of the octave he is reworking the featherbrained quotation of *U* 213). These mysteries (as well as others) begin to instruct Stephen effectively that he had better turn from the noise in the street to the bells in the church tower. To break out of that octave, that circling and inescapable 8 (my friend Father Robert Doran of the Marquette theology faculty suspects this is allied to Jung's possible entrapment in the mandala), so deeply operative for Joyce in his structuring of "Penelope" and the whole of *FW*, will require as I see the matter, a leap into the void beyond reason. "He is cured by faith who is sick of fate" (*FW* 482). *Ulysses* has 18 chapters, but *FW* has 17, and its final word (or potentially final word) affords the chance to leap into the void of a cosmic 8 turned on its side.

   4. Joyce wrote to Stanislaus from Rome in August 1906,

   I have just finished Dorian Grey [*sic*]. Some chapters are like Huysmans, catalogued atrocities, lists of perfumes and instruments. The central idea is fantastic. Dorian is exquisitely beautiful and becomes awfully wicked: but never ages. His portrait ages. I can imagine the capital which Wilde's prosecuting counsel made out of certain parts of it. It is not very difficult to read between the lines. Wilde seems to have had some good intentions in writing it—some wish to put himself before the world—but the book is rather crowded with lies and epigrams. If he had had the courage to develop the allusions in the book it might have been better. I suspect he has done this in some privately-printed books. Like his Irish imitator:

> Quite the reverse is
> The style of his verses

(Letters, 2:150)

The imitator, Ellmann notes, is Gogarty, who like Oscar went to Oxford and tried unsuccessfully to win first place in the Newdigate Prize competition, which Wilde had won. The likeness I see in Joyce's youthful view here, of Wilde hiding himself behind his ink rather than revealing his unique human experience in it, and in Joyce's mature view of Shem screening himself is that in both cases the ink is a veil for the personality. The difference I see is that in the discussion of Wilde above, Joyce is thinking of that veil as only a bad thing, a hindrance in getting at the truth behind the lies. The mature Joyce sees the veil as a necessary surface, like Prufrock's prepared face, which will express the deceptive nature of surfaces and will deceive only those who lack the faith and love to pierce to the dynamically operating symbol beneath. Such readers Joyce compares to nonbelievers who treat the appearance of the Eucharist as the whole thing, and thus make no contact with the divine reality operative beneath, as the blond rationalistic cop of *FW* 186 thinks it is ink (as it is), and misses the bottomless experience lying beneath.

5. Shaun accuses Shem of having stolen material from Shaun's own divine vocabulary: "Every dimmed letter in it is a copy and not a few of the silbils and wholly words I can show you in my Kingdom of Heaven" (*FW* 424). And Shem did this "As he was rising my lather" (*FW* 424-25), which seems to me identical with that lather from which Buck pretended to evoke Stephen-Christine. Further, Buck's stressing the *accidents* of Christ as present in the Eucharist—body and blood and 'ouns (the wounds that remained in his risen body as the cipher, according to Hopkins in the *Deutschland*, of infinite love operative in time and space) as well as his substantial form, his soul—sets up the contrast with Stephen's later dismissal of the body ("not indeed parcel of my body" [*U* 391]) and with Shem's "transaccidentated" instead of "transsubstantiated" on *FW* 186. The artist, unlike Christ in the Eucharist, loses his accidents so that his substance can enter into and humanize the ink.

6. Ellmann quotes Stephens's brief account of his first meeting with Joyce, in the course of which Joyce told Stephens "that my knowledge of Irish life was non-Catholic and so, non-existent" (*Ellmann,* p. 345).

7. Scotus points out that in the term "transmute," some common element remains before and after the change, as when hot wood becomes cold wood. So such a term is proper to accidental change, but not in a change from substance to another substance, where no common element remains: "Itaque vocabulum 'transsubstantiatio' melius in definitione usurpatur quam vocabulum 'transmutatio', quia in transmutatione materia communis remanere potest, ita ut nonnisi transitio secundum quid fiat, e.c. si lignum calidum in lignum frigidum mutatur. 'Substantiae in substantiam', id est non 'accidentis in accidens', quia, non est transaccidentatio, sed transssubstantiatio" (P. Parthenius Minges, O.F.M., *Joannis Duns Scoti Doctrina Philosophica et Theologica,* Tomus II [St. Bonaventure, 1930], p. 596).

8. "The Priesthoods of Stephen and Buck," *Approaches to Ulysses,* ed. Thomas F.

Staley and Bernard Benstock, (Pittsburgh, Pa.: University of Pittsburgh Press, 1970), p. 48.

9. Cf. "Swiftian Allegory and Dantean Parody in Joyce's 'Grace,' " *James Joyce Quarterly* 7, no. 1 (Fall 1969): 14.

10. Ithaca, N.Y.: Cornell University Press, 1972.

11. J. K. Huysmans, *Down There (La Bas), A Study in Satanism* trans. Keene Wallis (New York: University Books, 1958), p. 65.

12. Buck claimed in "Scylla and Charybdis" to give homage every day to the foamborn Aphrodite (*U* 201), but Bloom actually does every night honor, not the Greek mouth of which Buck speaks, but the triangle so significant in *FW* and which Bloom praises and recommends to Stephen (*U* 637) and which Buck had in the museum noted the pale Galilean eyes of Bloom searching out.

13. "If that is correct, I ask: If a 'transubstantiation' must be assumed in order that Christ's body may not be identified with the bread, why not also a 'transaccidentation,' in order that the body of Christ may not be identified with the accidents?" (*Luther's Works,* vol. 36, *Word and Sacrament,* no. 2, ed. Abdel Ross Wentz [Philadelphia: Fortress Press, 1959], p. 33). Like Wycliffe, Luther detested Aristotle, referring to him habitually as "the Monster." What Luther would think of *Finnegans Wake* might be guessed from the following lively passage: "There is now in vogue that song of the feast of Corpus Christi which is patched together from many passages of Scripture; in it the Scriptures are so forced and pulled in by the hair that God's worst enemy must have composed it, either that or it is the dream of a poor senseless idiot. Here Melchizedek is remembered, who offered bread and wine (Gen. 14:18); then the lamb comes into it which the people sacrificed of old (Exod. 12:5–6), and the cake of Elijah (I Kings 19:6), the manna of the fathers (Exod. 16:15), and Isaac, who was to be sacrificed (Gen. 22:2), and I don't know what has not been thought of. All these have had to serve as figures of the sacrament. It is a wonder that he did not include Baalam's ass (Num. 22:21) and David's mule (I Kings, 1:38); they could have had no less significance to the stupid ass than these other stories and figures" (ibid., 181–82).

14. I am inclined to think that this image operates in "I, huddled til summone be the massproduct of teamwork" (*FW* 546), where I take the "massproduct" to be allied to Bloom's cocoa and the "I" to be huddled here under the ink until some reader teams up with him and summons him forth.

15. *MND* 4. 1. 216 ff.

5. Joyce and the Jesuits

1. Vol. 171 (July–December), pp. 112–19. The reviewer was Shane Leslie.

2. Ibid., pp. 273–76. Excerpts from Leslie's and Martindale's reviews can be found in *James Joyce: The Critical Heritage,* ed. Robert H. Deming (New York: Barnes & Noble, 1970), pp. 200–206.

3. *The Workshop of Daedalus: James Joyce and the Raw Materials for A Portrait of the Artist as a Young Man,* comp. and ed. Robert Scholes and Richard M. Kain (Evanston, Ill.: Northwestern University Press, 1965), pp. 60–68. Hereafter *Workshop.*

4. *Jesuits*

They breed atheists
I learnt Latin prosody from the rhymes of Father Alvarez.
The nice terms of their philosophy are like the jargon of heraldry.
They are levites.

They do not love the end they serve.
The houses of jesuits are extraterritorial.
They flatter the wealthy but they do not love them nor their
ways. They flatter the clergy, their half brothers.
They who live by the mob shall perish by the mob.
They judge by categories.
Are they venal of speech because venality is the only point
of contact between pastor and flock?
They are erotically preoccuppied [sic]

(*Workshop* 102)

5. The bottom of Conmee's stroke, as he heads northeast to Artane, is appropriately spiritual, as his thoughts reach out southwest to Clongowes. See Leo Knuth, "A Bathymetric Reading of Joyce's *Ulysses*, Chapter X," *James Joyce Quarterly* 9, no. 4 (Summer 1972): 405–22. This appears also in his sparkling, insightful *The Wink of the Word* (Amsterdam: Rodopi, 1976), pp. 125–50, in somewhat different form.

6. *The Book as World: James Joyce's Ulysses* (Cambridge, Mass.: Harvard University Press, 1976).

7. *James Joyce: The Undiscover'd Country* (Dublin: Gill and Macmillan, 1977).

8. *The Journals and Papers of Gerard Manley Hopkins,* ed. Humphry House (London: Oxford University Press, 1959), p. 232. A note on p. 423 relates a reaction to Vaughan which, while considerably more dramatic than that of Conmee, may have had a similar psychic source: "This story is told of Hopkins (*Dublin Review,* Sept. 1920): 'Once at table he was seized with minor ecstasy at the conjunction of tartlets and Father Vaughan. He rose calling out: "Tartlets! tartlets! My kingdom for a tart. Bernard, I love you," and subsided into fantastic mirth.' "

9. William M. Schutte, *Joyce and Shakespeare, A Study in the Meaning of Ulysses* (New Haven, Conn.: Yale University Press, 1957): "The futility and the frustrations of her life were to be redeemed by Stephen's accession to the priesthood. When he loses his faith she quarrels with him like an older woman who sees her young lover slipping away from her. She even resorts to various ruses to hold him—his sister's ill health, a talk with her priest—but they only alienate him further. Thus he sees her deathbed appeal as only the last of her attempts to entrap his soul" (p. 108).

10. Ignatius's dancing is a famous anecdote among Jesuits, which Joyce would likely have heard many times in talks and retreats: "As the darkness of Saul was dispelled by the music of David, so Ortiz was restored to good spirits by Ignatius going through the cheerful steps of the folk dance of the Basques" (Robert Harvey, *Ignatius Loyola* [Milwaukee, Wis.: Bruce, 1936], p. 224).

11. (New York: Oxford University Press, 1972): "But Joyce is establishing a secret parallel and opposition: the body of God and the body of woman share blood in common. In allowing Molly to menstruate at the end Joyce consecrates the blood in the chamberpot rather than the blood in the chalice, mentioned by Mulligan at the beginning of the book. For this blood is substance, not more or less than substance. The great human potentiality is substantiation, not transsubstantiation, or sub-substantiation. It is this quality which the artist has too, in that he produces living human characters, not ethereal or less than human ones. It is human blood, not divine. Menstruation is Promethean" (p. 171).

12. Frank Budgen, *James Joyce and the Making of Ulysses* (Bloomington: Indiana University Press, 1967), p. 314.

13. J. F. Byrne, *Silent Years: An Autobiography with Memoirs of James Joyce and Our Ireland* (New York: Farrar, Straus and Young, 1953), p. 35.

14. *James Joyce and the Making of Ulysses,* p. 316.

15. "Next I will take an instance of modern times. If there be any set of men in the whole world who are railed against as the pattern of all that is evil, it is the Jesuit body. It is vain to ask their slanderers what they know of them; did they ever see a Jesuit? can they say whether there are many or few? what do they know of their teaching? 'Oh, it is quite *notorious,*' they reply: 'You might as well deny the sun in heaven; it is notorious that the Jesuits are a crafty, intriguing, unscrupulous, desperate, murderous, and exceedingly able body of men; a secret society, ever plotting against liberty, and government, and progress, and thought, and the prosperity of England. Nay, it is awful; they disguise themselves in a thousand shapes, as men of fashion, farmers, soldiers, labourers, butchers, and pedlars; they prowl about with handsome stocks, and stylish waistcoats, and gold chains about their persons, or in fustian jackets, as the case may be; and they do not hesitate to shed the blood of any one whatever, prince or peasant, who stands in their way.' Who can fathom the inanity of such statements?—which are made and therefore, I suppose, believed, not merely by the ignorant, but by educated men, who ought to know better, and will have to answer for their false witness. But all this is persisted in (John Henry Newman, *Lectures on The Present Position of Catholics in England* [Chicago: Loyola University Press, 1925], p. 16).

16. I have a discussion of these symbols in my *Metaphor in Hopkins* (Chapel Hill: University of North Carolina Press, 1961), chap. 4. On p. 100, where I quote the versicle and antiphon from the Office, I erred in stating my belief that this Office was the immediate source for Hopkins's symbols. The Office was not composed until early in the present century. What I should have said was that this Office, like Hopkins's use of the images, was drawn from a devotional tradition that often did link these images.

6. Joyce and Hopkins

1. *The Sermons and Devotional Writings of Gerard Manley Hopkins,* ed. Christopher Devlin (London: Oxford University Press, 1959), pp. 100–104. Some of the elements which I suspect do operate in Joyce's memory appear in this passage:

> The heart is one of these solid parts, of these pieces of flesh, and is a vessel of the liquid blood; it is an essential, a necessary part of the body, as no one will deny, it is found in Christ, was born with him, beat for 33 years in his breast, ceased beating at his death, was pierced by a lance after death upon the cross, and rose again with him at his resurrection with all other parts and members belonging to the perfection of the human body; it is therefore now in Christ's breast in heaven. And since, as I have said, everything in Christ is either godhead or united with the godhead, the heart, like all Christ's flesh, like Christ's whole body, like all Christ's human nature, is united with the godhead and deserves, requires, and must have paid to it, divine worship, that worship which is called in Greek λατρεία and is due to God alone. (P. 101)

2. Herbert Gorman, *James Joyce* (New York: Rinehart & Co., Inc., 1939): "The Faculty during Joyce's time (the famous Father Gerard Manley Hopkins was a member long before) was adequate but not exceptional" (p. 54). The note appended to Hopkins's name indicates that Gorman, and presumably Joyce (who in perhaps the funniest vision in *FW,* in a context mixing HCE with the pope and the general of the Jesuits and the Russian general, refers to his biography as "the Martyrology of

Gorman" [*FW* 349]), would not find the title of this chapter altogether inappropriate: "A year or so ago the contributor of University College Notes to a Dublin daily paper describing the ceremony of the extension or renovation of the Aula Maxima of the College wrote of it as 'hallowed by the memories of Cardinal Newman, Father Manley Hopkins and James Joyce' (!). The names, however, are not, from one point of view, incongruous."

3. *Metaphor in Hopkins* (Chapel Hill: University of North Carolina Press, 1961), p. 214. In "The Sea and the Skylark" Hopkins re-creates the music of the lark—

> Left hand, off land, I hear the lark ascend,
> His rash-fresh re-winded new-skeined score
> In crisps of curl off wild winch whirl, and pour
> And pelt music, till none's to spill nor spend.

Stephen speaks of his auguring birds: "But the notes were long and shrill and whirring, unlike the cry of vermin, falling a third or a fourth and trilled as the flying beaks clove the air. Their cry was shrill and clear and fine and falling like threads of silken light unwound from whirring spools" (*P* 493).

4. London: George Routledge and Sons Ltd. [1851].

5. Trench, *On the Study of Words*, p. 14.

6. Ibid., p. 9.

7. Joyce may have lifted one of his famous puns from the old bishop, who, in a careful paragraph on "trivial," points out: "Preparatory schools were called often 'trivial schools,' as occupying themselves with the 'trivium,' " ibid., p. 238.

8. *Sermons and Devotional Writings*, p. 118.

9. George Eliot, *Middlemarch* (Boston: Houghton Mifflin Co., 1956), bk. I, chap. 10, p. 62.

Index